lex & yacc

Nutshell Handbooks

Nutshell Handbooks are concise, down-to-earth books on a variety of UNIX topics. Other books of interest are:

Using C on the UNIX System   218 pages, $24.95

There are C programmers and there are UNIX programmers. The difference is the knowledge of the system calls and special library routines available on UNIX. This book is for intermediate to experienced C programmers who want to become UNIX system programmers.

lex & yacc   210 pages, $24.95

This handbook describes how to use *lex* and *yacc* to develop simple-to-use tools that can improve overall productivity for programmers working on UNIX.

Checking C Programs with lint   82 pages, $12.95

If your programs are to have a chance of being portable to UNIXes or to other C-capable computers besides the particular one you use, there are only two choices: use lint or keep your code to yourself. *lint* verifies C program segments against standard libraries; checks for common portability errors; tests code against guidelines. This handbook explains how to use *lint* effectively to improve C programs on UNIX.

Programming with curses   75 pages, $12.95

This handbook will help you make use of the *curses* library in your C programs. We have presented ample material on *curses* and its implementation in UNIX so that you understand the whole as well as its parts.

Managing Projects with make   83 pages, $12.95

This handbook provides a complete treatment of one of UNIX's most enduring contributions to software development, the *make* utility.

For orders or a free catalog of all our books, please contact us.

O'Reilly & Associates, Inc.

Creators and Publishers of Nutshell Handbooks
632 Petaluma Avenue, Sebastapol, CA 95472
1-800-338-6887 • in CA 1-800-533-6887 • or 1-707-829-0515
email: uunet!ora!nuts

lex & yacc

Tony Mason and Doug Brown

Editor
Dale Dougherty

O'Reilly & Associates, Inc.
632 Petaluma Avenue
Sebastopol, CA 95472

lex & yacc
by Tony Mason and Doug Brown

Acquisitions Editor: Tim O'Reilly

Developmental Editor: Dale Dougherty

Printing History

May 1990:   First printing.

While every precaution has been taken in the preparation of this book, the publisher assumes no responsibility for errors or omissions, or for damages resulting from the use of the information contained herein.

Please address comments and questions in care of the publisher:

O'Reilly & Associates, Inc.
632 Petaluma Avenue
Sebastopol, CA 95472
in USA 1-800-338-6887 in CA 1-800-533-6887
international +1 707-829-0515

UUCP: uunet!ora!nuts
Internet: nuts@ora.com

TABLE OF CONTENTS

Chapter 6 A Reference for Lex Specifications

Chapter 7 A Reference for Yacc Specifications

Chapter 8 Ambiguities and Conflicts in Yacc Grammars

Chapter 9 Error Reporting and Recovery

Appendix A Lex Options and Error Messages

Appendix B Yacc Options and Error Messages

Appendix C GNU Bison

Figures

Examples

Tables

Preface

Scope of this Book
Availability of Lex and Yacc
Sample Programs
Conventions Used in this Handbook
Acknowledgements

Lex and yacc are tools designed for writers of compilers and interpreters, although there are a wider range of applications that will interest the noncompiler writer. Lex and yacc can be used for a variety of very useful tasks; more importantly, they provide rapid prototyping, easy modification, and simple maintenance. To stimulate your imagination, here are a few initial suggestions for things you could use lex and yacc to develop:

- A desktop calculator.
- A typesetting system for generating *real* typesetter output.
- A C compiler.
- A lexical analyzer.
- A menu compiler.
- A screen generator.

This must seem a rather diverse list, yet many existing UNIX utilities were built using lex and yacc. For example, the UNIX compiler *bc* is just such a desktop calculator. It offers functions, variables, and many of the features necessary for a sophisticated scientific calculator. Further, the UNIX typesetting tools, *troff* and *nroff*, demonstrate just such a typesetting system. Both *pcc*, the *portable C compiler*, and the GNU project's C compilers are samples of C compilers which rely upon yacc. Indeed, lex itself was constructed using a yacc grammar!

In Figure 1, we provide a graphic comparison of the power of various tools in the UNIX programming toolkit; lex and yacc are powerful indeed but still provide the programmer with tools not so complex as C itself.

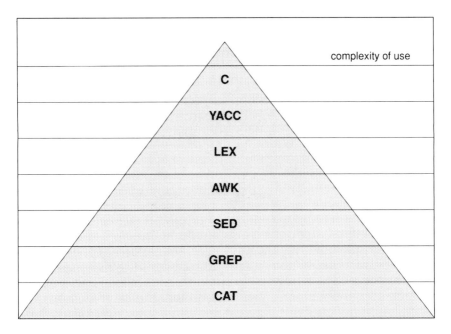

Figure   1. Hierarchy of UNIX tools

Scope of this Book

Chapter 1, *Introduction to Lex and Yacc*, gives an overview of how and why lex and yacc are used to create compilers and interpreters. It also introduces basic terms we use throughout the book.

Chapter 2, *The Mechanics of Lex and Yacc*, describes how to use lex and yacc. It details how to write the specification files for these programs and how to generate executable code.

Chapter 3, *Building a Calculator*, gives a full example of using lex and yacc by developing a simple desktop calculator.

Chapter 4, *The MGL*, demonstrates how to use lex and yacc to develop a menu generator.

Chapter 5, *The SGL*, details the development of an even more complex example, that of a screen generator.

Chapter 6, *A Reference for Lex Specifications*, and Chapter 7, *A Reference for Yacc Specifications*, provide detailed descriptions of the various options available to the lex and yacc programmer. These chapters and the two that follow provide the technical information necessary for the now experienced lex and yacc programmer's use while developing new applications programs that use lex and yacc.

Chapter 8, *Ambiguities and Conflicts in Yacc Grammars*, explains what yacc ambiguities and conflicts are and then develops methods that can be used to locate and correct such problems.

Chapter 9, *Error Reporting and Recovery*, discusses some mechanisms that can be used by the compiler or interpreter designer in locating, recognizing, and reporting errors from the input of the compiler user.

Appendix A, *Lex Options and Error Messages*, describes the command line syntax of lex and the error messages it reports.

Appendix B, *Yacc Options and Error Messages*, describes the command line syntax of yacc and lists errors reported by yacc. It provides examples of code which can cause such errors and suggests possible solutions to the errors.

Appendix C, *GNU Bison*, discusses differences found in the Free Software Foundation's implementation of yacc.

Appendix D, *GNU Flex*, discusses differences found in the Free Software Foundation's implementation of lex.

Appendix E, *MGL Compiler Code*, provides the complete source code for the menu generation language compiler discussed in Chapter 4.

The *Glossary* lists technical terms, most of which relate to language and compiler theory.

The *Bibliography* lists other documentation on lex and yacc, as well as helpful books on compiler design.

We presume the reader is familiar with C, as most examples are in C, lex, or yacc, with the remainder being in the special purpose languages developed within the text itself.

Availability of Lex and Yacc

Lex and yacc were both developed at Bell Laboratories in the 1970s. Yacc was the first of the two, developed by Stephen C. Johnson. Lex was designed to work with yacc by M. E. Lesk and E. Schmidt. Both lex and yacc have been standard UNIX utilities since Version 7, and there are no significant differences between Berkeley and System V versions. The articles written by the developers remain the primary source of information on lex and yacc.

The GNU Project of the Free Software Foundation distributions *bison*, a yacc replacement; *bison* was written by Robert Corbett and Richard Stallman. The *bison* manual, written by Charles Donnelly and Richard Stallman, is excellent, especially for referencing specific features. Appendix C discusses the differences between yacc and *bison*.

The GNU Project also distributes *flex* (*Fast Lexical Analyzer Generator), "a rewrite of lex intended to right some of that tool's deficiencies," according to its reference page. *flex* was originally written by Jef Poskanzer; Vern Paxson and Van Jacobson are named as authors of the current version. Appendix D covers differences between lex and *flex*.

There is at least one version of lex and yacc available for DOS machines. MKS (Mortice Kern Systems Inc.), publishers of the MKS Toolkit, offers lex and yacc as a separate product that supports many PC C compilers. MKS lex and yacc comes with a very good manual.

Sample Programs

All samples in this book were written and tested under UNIX on various systems running BSD 4.2 and 4.3, as well as System V. They should work under other operating systems, but it may require some work on the part of the reader to make them do so. The yacc grammars have been tested with GNU *bison*, and the lex specifications have been tested with GNU *flex*. For more information on *bison* and *flex*, see Appendices C and D.

The full-length sample programs in this book are available free of charge from UUNET (that is, except for UUNET's connect-time charges). If you have access to UUNET, you can retrieve the source code using *uucp* or *ftp*.

For uucp transfer, the filename is *˜/uucp/nutshell/lexyacc/progs.tar .Z*. For ftp transfer, *cd* to */nutshell/lexyacc*, specify binary transfer, and get *progs.tar.Z*. You will need to *uncompress* the files and extract them from the archive with:

```
tar xvf filename
```

Conventions Used in this Handbook

The following conventions are used in this book:

Bold   is used for statements and functions, identifiers, and program names.

Italic   is used for file and directory names when they appear in the body of a paragraph as well as for data types and to emphasize new terms and concepts when they are introduced.

`Constant Width`   is used in examples to show the contents of files or the output from commands.

`Constant Bold`   is used in examples to show command lines and options that should be typed literally by the user.

Quotes   are used to identify a code fragment in explanatory text. System messages, signs, and symbols are quoted as well.

$ is the Bourne Shell prompt.

[]   surround optional elements in a description of program syntax. (The brackets themselves should never be typed.)

Acknowledgements

This book began with Tony Mason's MGL and SGL compilers. Tony developed most of the material in this book, working with Dale Dougherty to make it a "Nutshell." Doug Brown contributed Chapter 8, *Ambiguities and Conflicts in Yacc Grammars*. Dale wrote Chapter 2, *The Mechanics of Lex and Yacc*, and revised portions of the book. Tim O'Reilly made it a better book by withholding his editorial blessing until he found what he was looking for in the book. Thanks to Butch Anton, Ed Engler, and Mike Loukides for their comments on technical content. Thanks also to John W. Lockhart for reading a draft with an eye for stylistic issues. And thanks to Chris Reilly for his work on the graphics. Finally, Ruth Terry brought the book into print with her usual diligence and her sharp eye for every editorial detail. Though she was trying to work odd hours to also care for her family, it seemed she was caring for this book all hours of the day.

1

Introduction to
Lex and Yacc

Compilers and Interpreters
Lexical Analysis
A Parser
Abstract Machines

Lex and yacc are tools that help you create C routines that analyze and interpret an input stream. They can be used to help write compilers and interpreters or any program whose input has a well-defined structure.

Lex reads a specification file containing regular expressions for pattern matching and generates a C routine that performs lexical analysis. This routine reads a stream of characters and matches sequences that identify *tokens*. For instance, a calculator must be able to distinguish operators and operands. Yacc reads a specification file that codifies the grammar of a language and generates a parsing routine. This routine groups tokens into meaningful sequences and invokes action routines to act upon them. The calculator, for example, must recognize a complete expression, then evaluate it and print the result.

In this chapter, we look at the functions performed by a lexical analyzer and a parser in developing compilers and interpreters. We describe why lex and yacc are used and give an overview of how they actually work. Finally, we describe the abstract machines that implement the lexical analyzer and parser created by lex and yacc.

Compilers and Interpreters

A compiler takes a description of a process (i.e., a program) and converts it into a set of instructions that can be performed by the computer. Figure 1-1 shows the typical model of operation used by the compiler. The user creates a text file that contains the program source code; the compiler receives this file as input and converts the program into object code, a series of instructions that can be executed by the computer.

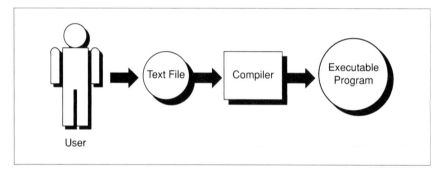

Figure 1-1. Flow diagram of a compiler

Language compilers can be built for full-scale programming languages or for "little languages" that serve a specialized function. The input for a compiler typically spans multiple lines; it typically comes from a file that is created using an editor or generated by another computer program.

In comparison, an interpreter does not have the intermediate stages of a text file or an executable program. In the interpreter, each independent instruction is processed as received directly from the user. Any command line interpreter acts immediately upon the user's typed input. A calculator is such an example.

Neither the compiler nor the interpreter is better than the other. Each one is useful depending upon the type and complexity of the problem. In this book, we create both an interpreter (an interactive calculator) and a compiler (a menu/screen generation language compiler). The calculator is a simple but useful tool for everyday tasks. The menu generation language is a compiler that allows you to enter a simple description of a menu and generate a C program which, when compiled, creates a menu-style front-end.

Compilers and interpreters are very similar in how they process input and generate output. (From this point on, we will use compiler to mean both compilers and interpreters.) The input to a compiler is a character stream, and the output is some action or series of actions, perhaps as simple as printing each character that is typed by the user.

The compiler performs its tasks in three stages:

- The first stage consists of a *lexical analyzer* whose job it is to scan the input and convert sequences of characters into tokens. Tokens are essentially classifications of groups of characters. A series of alphabetic characters forms a word; a series of digits forms a number.

- In the second stage, a parser reads tokens and assembles them into language constructs. For instance, the constructs of a programming language describe how keywords, identifiers, and expressions can be combined to form statements.

- The third stage, acting upon the input, is done by code supplied by the compiler writer.

Logically, each stage prepares the input for the next stage. Thus, the operating system provides the byte stream, the lexical analyzer provides the grouping of bytes into tokens, the parser provides the grouping of tokens into statements within the language, and the actions provide interpretation for the tokens' values. This simple model of compilation is illustrated in Figure 1-2.

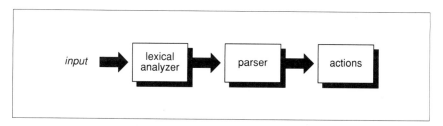

Figure 1-2. Basic model of processing for interpreters and compilers

You could write a custom lexical analyzer or parser in any computer language. Despite the ability of such general purpose languages as C, lex and yacc are more flexible and far less complex to use. Typically it does not makes sense to use anything else.

Lex generates the C code for a lexical analyzer, and yacc generates the code for a parser. Both lex and yacc take as their input a specification file which is typically shorter than a custom program and more easily read and understood. By convention, the suffix of the lex specification file is *.l* and for the yacc specification file is *.y*. The output of lex and yacc is C source code. Lex creates a routine named **yylex** in a file named *lex.yy.c*. Yacc creates a routine named **yyparse** in a file named *y.tab.c*.

These routines are combined with user-supplied C source code, which is typically placed in a separate file but could be placed in the yacc specification file. The user-supplied code usually consists of a **main** routine that calls **yyparse**, which in turn calls **yylex**. All of these routines must be compiled, and in most cases, the lex and yacc libraries must be loaded at compile time. These libraries contain a number of supporting routines that are required, if not supplied, by the user. A diagram illustrating the steps in developing a new program using lex and yacc is shown in Figure 1-3.

Now we can turn to looking at developing the specifications for lexical and parsing routines and understanding how they work.

Lexical Analysis

Input streams in UNIX are byte streams. Converting the byte stream into a token stream is the task of a lexical routine.

The program shown in Example 1-1 demonstrates a hand-coded lexical analyzer. This program contains a lexical routine named **lexer** which reads characters from input and, when it matches a token, returns the symbol identifying the token. The **main** routine calls **lexer** and prints the symbol it returns.

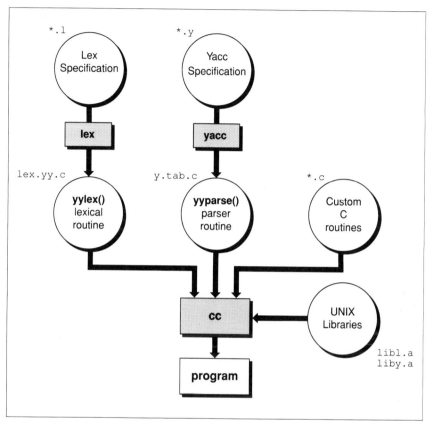

Figure 1-3. Using lex and yacc

Example 1-1. Sample C lexical analyzer

```
#include <stdio.h>
#include <ctype.h>
char *progname;

#define NUMBER 400
#define COMMENT 401
#define TEXT 402
#define COMMAND 403

main(argc,argv)
int argc;
```

Example 1-1. Sample C lexical analyzer (continued)

```
char *argv[];
{
int val;

while(val = lexer()) printf("value is %d\n",val);
}

lexer()
{
    int c;

    while ((c=getchar()) == ' ' || c == '\t')
        ;
    if (c == EOF)
        return 0;
    if (c == '.' || isdigit(c)) {      /* number */
        while ((c = getchar()) != EOF && isdigit(c));
if(c == '.') while ((c = getchar()) != EOF && isdigit(c));
        ungetc(c, stdin);
        return NUMBER;
    }
    if ( c == '#' ) { /* comment */
        int index = 1;
        while ((c = getchar()) != EOF && c != '\n');
        ungetc(c,stdin);
        return COMMENT;
    }
    if ( c == '"' ) { /* literal text */
        int index = 1;
        while ((c = getchar()) != EOF &&
        c != '"' && c != '\n');
        if(c == '\n') ungetc(c,stdin);
        return TEXT;
    }
    if ( isalpha(c)) { /* check to see if it is a command */
        int index = 1;

        while ((c = getchar()) != EOF && isalnum(c));
        ungetc(c, stdin);
        return COMMAND;
    }
    return c;
}
```

This sample program examines the input stream and groups individual characters
into several distinct tokens: numbers, commands, strings, and comments.
Although our sample is not complex, it demonstrates that even such a small
parser is not simple. Someone not familiar with the operation of this program
would spend a few minutes examining it to determine what it was actually doing.

By comparison, the lex specification shown in Example 1-2 is functionally identical and less obtuse.

Example 1-2. Sample lex lexical analyzer

```
%{
#define NUMBER 400
#define COMMENT 401
#define TEXT 402
#define COMMAND 403
%}
%%
[ \t]+                     ;
[0-9]+                |
[0-9]+\.[0-9]+        |
\.[0-9]+                  { return NUMBER; }
#*                        { return COMMENT; }
\"[^\"\n]*\"              { return TEXT; }
[a-zA-Z][a-zA-Z0-9]+     { return COMMAND; }
\n                        { return '\n'; }
%%
#include <stdio.h>

main(argc,argv)
int argc;
char *argv[];
{
int val;

while(val = yylex()) printf("value is %d\n",val);
}
```

The code size of the lex example is about one-third the size of the C version. Rest assured that as the size of the grammar to be examined grows, this dramatic difference will increase even further in favor of lex. Aside from the issue of the amount of code that the programmer must write (which is significant) is that of the final output size. For our samples, the difference between the C version and the lex version was 1024 bytes.*

A lex specification for a lexical analyzer contains a set of rules for matching tokens and one or more C action statements that are performed when a token is matched. The pattern matching rules are expressed in UNIX regular expression syntax. Indeed, a lex specification is remarkably similar to an *awk* script; however, actions are written in C and are not interpreted by lex but by the C compiler.

---

*This was on a Digital Vaxstation II running BSD 4.3. Much of the lex overhead, however, is of a fixed size. Thus, as the lexical analyzer size increases and the corresponding complexity of the C version of it does as well, the lex output version will change far less.

For example, if we wished to construct a lexical analyzer for C, the specification would include rules to match built-in keywords such as **if** and **char**. Similarly, it would also include rules to match other tokens such as identifiers, which in C are used for variables and function names.

Regular Expressions

Regular expressions provide a tremendous amount of flexibility in many situations. Many UNIX programs, including *awk*, *sed*, and *vi*, make use of regular expressions for pattern matching. We assume that you are basically familiar with UNIX regular expression syntax. We will, however, review a few examples in this chapter and provide more information in Chapter 6, *A Reference for Lex Specifications*. See also the sidebar "What is a Language?" for a more formal definition of regular expressions.

Let's look at an example of a regular expression. Suppose that we wanted to match any of the following numbers:

```
100
1.1
1
11.10
```

The following regular expression would do:

```
([0-9]*\.)*[0-9]+
```

We can break this regular expression up into two parts. Let's look at the second part first:

```
[0-9]+
```

Brackets ([]) enclose a set of exclusive choices; a consecutive range of letters or digits within brackets can be abbreviated by the use of a "-". Here the expression specifies any single digit from 0 through 9. "+" means one or more of the preceding. Thus, this part of the expression matches "1" or "100" or any sequence of digits. Here is the first part:

```
([0-9]*\.)*
```

"*" means zero or more of the preceding. Parentheses, (), can be used to group an expression so that it can be modified as a single unit. The asterisk following the expression in parentheses makes the presence of this entire expression optional. Similarly, the asterisk following "[0-9]" makes the digits preceding the decimal point optional. Notice that the decimal point itself is escaped by a backslash; the dot (.) matches any character except newline, and the backslash (\) is used to escape the special meaning of metacharacters so that they can be interpreted literally. Thus, this part of the expression matches a decimal point preceded by any sequence of digits.

Actions

The basic function of the lexical routine is to match a token and return a *token number* to the parser routine that called it. The token number is defined by a symbol that the parser uses to identify a token. In addition, the lexical routine can pass the actual value of the token itself.

The actions in a lex specification consist of C language statements that return the token number and its value. The token numbers are defined by yacc when it processes the tokens declared in the yacc specification. The **#define** statement is used to define the token numbers:

```
#define NUMBER 257
```

These symbol definitions are output in *y.tab.c*, along with the **yyparse** routine. (Each ASCII character is defined as a token whose number is its ASCII value (0 to 256); thus, user-defined tokens begin at 257.) The parser and the lexical routine must use the same set of symbols to identify tokens; therefore the lexical routine must have access to the symbols defined by the parser. One way to do it is to tell yacc to create the header file *y.tab.h* that can be included in the lex specification. Of course, you could explicitly define these symbols in the lex specification, as was shown in Example 1-2, making sure they correspond to the token numbers assigned in yacc.

To return the token number in an action, use the **return** statement. For example, here is a rule that matches any number and the action returns the token **NUMBER**:

```
[0-9]+          { return NUMBER; }
```

Passing the value of the token to the parser is more work. Lex creates an external variable named **yytext** that contains the string of characters that are matched by the regular expression. An external variable named **yylval** is set up by yacc to pass the token value from the lexical analyzer to the parser. The type of **yylval** is an *int*, by default. Therefore, to assign the value of **yytext** to **yylval**, you must convert this value from a string to an *int*. You can change the type of **yylval** or, as we'll see later on, define a union of multiple data types for **yylval**.

For instance, you could use the **atoi** function to convert a number stored as a string in **yytext** to an *int* and assign it to **yylval**:

```
[0-9]+          {   yylval = atoi(yytext);
                    return NUMBER;
                }
```

The value of **yylval** is then available for the parser's action routines.

Finally, once the lexical routine detects an end-of-file, it must return 0 to the parser.

A Parser

The lexical analyzer generates a stream of tokens for the parser to interpret. The parser organizes the tokens it reads according to the rules of a grammar. For instance, a grammar for a programming language describes the input structure of a program; it needs a rule describing a statement. When the parser has a sequence of tokens that corresponds to a rule, an associated action is executed. The actions can make use of the values of tokens to generate output or pass the value to other routines in the program.

The Elements of a Grammar

The syntax of a program can be defined by a *context-free grammar*. A context-free grammar is essentially a hierarchical structure that indicates the relationships of various language constructs. The most common notation used to describe a context-free grammar is known as BNF (Backus-Naur Form). The input to yacc closely follows BNF.

The description of this grammar is in the form of *production rules*. Such production rules simply consist of a rule followed by its definition. The definition consists of symbols which are *nonterminals* in that they point to other rules or *terminals* that correspond to tokens. These are sometimes also called the left-hand side, which must be a nonterminal, and the right-hand side, which can be zero or more nonterminals and terminals. For example, here is a simple grammar:

```
list ← object I list object
object ← string I number
string ← text I comment I command
number ← number I +number I -number I number.number
```

In this example, the boldfaced words represent the terminals and the remaining words are the nonterminals. The first rule:

```
list ← object I list object
```

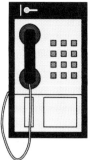

The *lingua franca* of a Pay Phone

To understand what a parser does, let's describe it by analogy to a pay telephone. To place a call, it costs 20 cents, and that 20 cents can be paid using nickels and dimes. Each coin represents one token. The syntax of our language must state what combinations of tokens make up 20 cents. The following rules describe these combinations:

For example, if the first coin is a nickel and the second coin is a dime, we do not yet have a valid combination, and to produce one, we need a third coin that is a nickel. Each of these lines can be considered rules for producing a valid combination totaling exactly 20 cents. The "machine" is able to apply these rules by "ruling out" the ones that are no longer valid. For instance, if the first coin is a dime, we know that only the last two rules can be applied. If the next coin is a nickel, then only the fourth rule is left to be applied on remaining input. Parsing, then, is the ability to recognize certain sequences of tokens.

The above set of rules have the same action associated with them, which might be "connect caller." We could write rules to recognize other tokens and to specify different actions. For instance, we might have a rule for pennies and slugs, dropping the token into the coin return slot. Similarly, we could have a rule:

and specify an action that returns the nickel and makes the connection. (This, of course, is not a *real* pay phone.) The set of rules constitute a *grammar*. In other words, a grammar describes the combinations of tokens that produce meaningful results.

states that a *list* is made up either of an *object* or of a *list* and an *object*. Fundamentally, then, this is a shorthand for two possible rules:

list ← object
list ← list object

The second form of the rule is a *recursive* definition. This allows a complex concept, like a list, to be described in a compact form. Since we do not know in advance how many elements of this list there will be, we could not conveniently define what a list was without this recursive form. Simply put, this definition states that a list is a sequence of objects, one after the other. Were we to describe this as a comma-separated list, the rule would become:

list ← object I list ','object

The I is a *union* operator. Note, for example, its use in the last rule:

number ← **number** I **+number** I **-number** I **number.number**

Thus, a number is either a **number** (note the boldfacing indicates it is the *terminal* **number**, not the rule *number*), a **number** with a plus (+) in front, a **number** with a minus (-) in front, or two **numbers** separated by a decimal point (.). Thus, many possible choices may be listed in a compact form.

The construction of a grammar is a bottom-up process, including each grouping in larger groupings until there is a single top-level grouping that includes all other groupings. This top-level construct is referred to as the *start* symbol. In our sample grammar above, "list" is the start symbol. When the start symbol is recognized and there is no more input, then the parser knows it has seen a complete program. The parser created by yacc returns 0 if all the input is valid and 1 if a syntax error has been encountered.

A parser can do more than simply recognize the correct syntax for a program. A parser can be designed to recognize erroneous sequences and issue reasonable error messages; for example, the C compiler's recognition that a character string is not terminated by a closing quotation (") character.

A Yacc Grammar

A yacc specification for a grammar consists of production rules and actions. Yacc processes this specification and creates the source code for a parsing routine.

Let's look at how the lexical routine and the parser work together by analyzing a small fragment of C code:

```
if (i)
    return(i);
```

The lexical analyzer converts this stream of bytes into tokens by recognizing particular patterns. For instance, when the lexical analyzer sees "return (i)", it might recognize the following elements:

```
return          token RETURN
(               literal '('
i               token ID
)               literal ')'
```

If the lexical analyzer sees "i" and it fails to match any built-in command, it would return the token **ID** to the parser; the parser might pass the variable name to an action routine that could look it up in a symbol table to determine if the identifier was valid. Thus, each pattern constitutes a token, which, in turn, is processed by the parser.

The yacc specification might have the following rule to define a valid statement:

```
stmt:   RETURN expr ';'
        ;
```

The token **RETURN** is a terminal symbol identified by the lexical analyzer. **expr** is a nonterminal symbol defined by a grammar rule. Here is a rule for **expr**:

```
expr:       ID
        |   '(' expr ')'
        ;
```

The vertical bar (|) indicates that there are alternate definitions for the same rule. This rule states that an **expr** can be an ID or an ID within parentheses.

Any grammar rule can have an action associated with it to evaluate the tokens that were recognized. Like lex, an action is one or more C statements that can perform a variety of tasks, including producing output or altering external variables. Frequently, the action acts upon the value of the tokens in the construct.

Recall that the lexical analyzer assigned the value of each token to the external variable **yylval**. Yacc provides a positional notation for accessing the value of a token in an expression:

```
expr:   NUM '+' NUM          { printf("%d",$1 + $3); }
```

In this case, the action prints the sum of the value of the first and third tokens. The value returned by an action can be assigned to the variable "$$". Look at the following example:

```
expr:       ID                { $$ = $1; }
     | '(' expr ')'           { $$ = $2; }
     ;
```

The first action is invoked when "ID" is recognized, returning the value of the token **ID**. Actually, this is the default action, and it need not be specified. The second action selects the value of **expr** as the second element in the construct.

Summary of Lexical and Parsing Routines

We have discussed how **yylex**, the lexical routine created by lex, and **yyparse**, the parsing routine produced by yacc, work together. Look at Figure 1-4 which illustrates the flow of control in lexical and parsing routines.

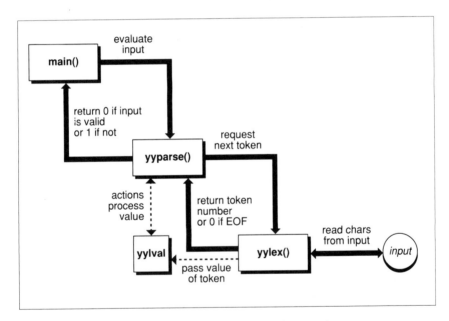

Figure 1-4. Flow of control in lexical and parsing routines

A **main** routine invokes **yyparse** to evaluate whether or not the input is valid. **yyparse** invokes a routine named **yylex** each time it needs a token. (**yylex** can be hand-coded or generated by lex.) This lexical routine reads the input stream, and for each token that it matches, it returns the token number to the parser. The lexical routine can also pass the value of the token using the external variable **yylval**. The parser's action routines can make use of this value as well as other user-supplied routines. The action routines can create the output generated by the program, although not necessarily exclusively.

When the lexical routine has exhausted the input, it returns a 0 to the parser. If the parser has recognized the **start** rule, the top-level in the grammar's hierarchical structure, then the parser returns 0, meaning that the input was valid. If at any time it receives a token number or a sequence of tokens that it does not recognize or if the lexical routine returns 0 before a start symbol has been recognized, then the parser returns 1, reporting a syntax error.

Abstract Machines

To fully understand the operations of lex and yacc, it is useful to know more about the abstract machines on which the lexical analyzer and the parser are based. In this section, we describe these machines and how they function.

Finite Automata

Lex takes a set of regular expressions and a description of what to do when the regular expression is detected; from this, it builds a *finite automaton* in C. A finite automaton is a good model for programmers, because such a machine is very simple to describe and understand and, most importantly, can be implemented on a real computer to run quickly and efficiently.

A finite automaton is an abstract machine consisting of a finite set of states and transitions from state to state, based upon the input symbols chosen from the alphabet Σ. There is exactly one starting state and a set of terminal states. Each state is either an *accepting state* or a *nonaccepting state*. The finite automaton begins in the *initial state* and examines the first input token. For lex, a token corresponds to the next character. The machine then moves to the next state based upon that token.

To demonstrate a finite automaton graphically, we have constructed a state diagram (in Figure 1-5) of a simple finite state machine designed to accept a real number without an exponent. Using regular expression syntax, such a number can be expressed as follows:

```
[0-9]*(.[0-9]+)?
```

The machine to tokenize this input has four states and six transitions. We will call the four states s_0, s_1, s_2, and s_3. The initial state is s_0, and the accepting state is s_1. Now we can define the *transition function* to be the function that maps the current state, plus the current input token, to a new state. Thus, to traverse the machine, we continue to feed new tokens, along with the current state, into the transition function to determine the next state. If there are no transitions out of the current state with the current input (say, for instance, an extra decimal point is seen, rather than a digit), the finite automaton does *not accept* the input. If there is no more input and the finite automaton is in an *accepting* state, the finite automaton *accepts* the input. If there is no more input and the finite automaton is *not* in an *accepting* state, the finite automaton does *not accept* the input.

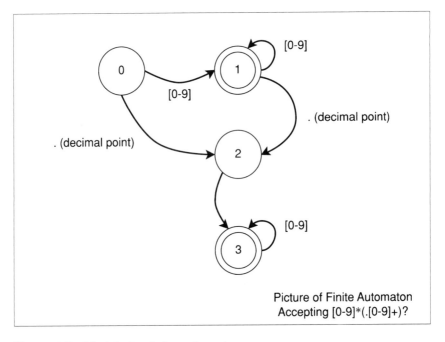

Picture of Finite Automaton
Accepting [0-9]*(.[0-9]+)?

Figure 1-5. Model of a finite automaton

In Figure 1-5, the finite automaton's transition function can be described as a set of triples (**initial_state, input_token, new_state**), as follows:

$(s_0, [0-9], s_1)$
$(s_0, ., s_2)$
$(s_1, [0-9], s_1)$
$(s_1, ., s_2)$
$(s_2, [0-9], s_3)$
$(s_3, [0-9], s_3)$

where the *accepting states* are s_1 and s_3. The figure, as well as the formal state description, is *equivalent* to the regular expression. One reason finite state machines, such as the one above, are important is that they are equivalent to regular expressions. That is, any regular expression can be recognized by a finite state machine (the converse is also true).* It is this property that allows lex to take the regular-expression-based lexical analyzer description and build a finite state machine in C. Finite state machines are less powerful than Turing machines (the type of machine all computer languages can "implement"), so the task is possible (although still not trivial).

Aside from explaining *why* lex can even work, the description of the state machine is a very useful tool. State machines, independent of lex, appear in many places: communication protocols, device drivers, and even applications programs. For the lex user, the visual model of the finite state machine is an invaluable debugging tool, as well as an aid for gaining an insight into *what* the specific lex grammar is doing.

Of course, it is not necessary to construct the finite state machine for each lex input file, but when the lex input file has become quite complex, it can be useful to provide an alternative model of what precisely is happening inside. In fact, it is possible to use lex and yacc to generate a program which will create the finite state model (visually, or as a mathematical description) of the lexical analyzer.

There are many other interesting properties of finite automata. One potentially important one is that *nondeterministic* finite automata (those that have ε transitions and multiple transitions on a particular input) are equivalent to deterministic finite automata. The deterministic version, however, can have exponentially more states than the nondeterministic version. Hence, the warning in the original lex paper:

> There are pathological expressions which produce exponential growth of the tables when converted to deterministic machines; fortunately, they are rare.

---

*The actual proof of this assertion is nontrivial, so it is omitted here, but it is available elsewhere (e.g., *Introduction to Automata Theory, Languages, and Computation*, by Hopcroft and Jeffrey D. Ullman, Addison-Wesley, 1979, pp. 30-32).

What is a Language?

What do we mean by the term *language*? Formally, a language is always recognized over an *alphabet*, which is just a set of symbols, such as the ASCII characters or the binary numbers. For the sake of simplicity, binary numbers are often used because any larger, finite alphabet is equivalent (since a series of zeros and ones can represent each ASCII character—just as they, in fact, do for digital computers). We will use Σ to represent the alphabet. A *string* is a sequence of characters from the alphabet. The term Σ* represents all possible strings. Finally, we can define a language. A *language* is a subset of Σ*.

For example, suppose $\Sigma = \{0,1\}$ (the binary alphabet). Σ* represents all possible strings of zeros and ones. If our language $L = \{0,1,10,11\}$, then we can say L is a language over Σ. It is important to note that a language need not be *finite* and indeed will often not be so. Just to prove our point, we offer yet another example. If Σ = ASCII Alphabet and $L = \{x | x = \#\alpha, \alpha \in \Sigma\}$, the language L is *infinite*. Yet this language describes comments as used in the UNIX command shells!

Lex works with a small class of languages called the *regular languages*. A language is *regular* if it can be described by a *regular expression*. We can define a regular expression recursively:

1. ε (the *empty* string) is a regular expression.

2. For each element $a \in \Sigma$ (*a* is an element of the alphabet), *a* is a regular expression.

3. If *a* and *b* are regular expressions, then $a + b$, $a * b$, and a* are regular expressions. Denote *union* as +, *concatenation* as *, and *closure* as *. By *union*, we mean the union of the sets. Thus, (01) + (10) denotes either the string "01" or the string "10". By *concatenation*, we mean the product of the sets. Thus, (01) * (10) denotes the string "0110". By *closure*, we mean the concatenation of zero or more copies of the specified set. Thus, (01)* denotes the empty string "ε" (that is, zero repetitions of the string), "01", "0101", and so forth.

Pushdown Automata

Finite automata are limited because they have no concept of *past state*. Hence, the automaton is unable to use any knowledge of what the *previous* token was. This will make recognition of some languages impossible. For instance, the language of nested comments in C cannot be recognized by any finite state machine (a complete proof is located in "Rules Section" in Chapter 6, *A Reference for Lex Specifications*). Fundamentally, this stems from the inability of the machine to count. Another example would be the language of all palindromes (a word or phrase that reads the same backward or forward, e.g., level) in the ASCII alphabet. Such a language cannot be recognized by a finite state machine.*

A pushdown automaton is similar to the finite automaton. It has a finite number of states, a transition function, and an input stream. The difference is that the pushdown automaton is equipped with a *stack*. The transition function works on the initial state, the current top element of the stack, and the current input token, yielding the new state.

Although this might seem to be a small change, it essentially solves the earlier problem referred to in both the nested comment and the palindrome examples. The machine, informally speaking, can push each opening symbol onto the stack and pull it off when it sees the closing symbol.

This added capability makes the pushdown automaton more useful. For example, this ability to recall past state allows yacc to recognize its grammars, known as the LALR(1) class of languages.† The LALR(1) languages are essentially a class of languages containing context dependency upon no more than a single token.

Each time yacc reads a token, it pushes it on the stack. The stack is known as the parser stack, and the pushing of a token on it is called *shifting*. For instance, if we look at our earlier example of the return statement, suppose that two tokens have been read. The parser stack has the following contents:

```
(
return
```

The next token is **ID**, and it is shifted to the stack. However, because it makes up an **expr**, this element can be reduced to the rule **expr**, which replaces it on the stack. Similarly, when the next token ")" is read, the first three elements of the stack are popped off the stack and replaced by **expr**. When the semicolon is

---

*This is a general case of the nested comments argument. Specifically, the language of nested comments is contained in the language of all palindromes; hence, the language of all palindromes cannot be regular.

†*LookAhead Left Recursive* languages that can look ahead one token are very similar to a class of languages called the *context-free grammars*.

recognized, **return** and **expr** are popped off the stack and replaced by **stmt**. By shifting tokens on the parser stack and reducing them as syntactical groupings are recognized, the parser attempts to reduce all input down to the grammar's **start** symbol.

Yacc is not able to process all grammars; that functionality is left for *Turing machines*—abstract machines with a finite set of instructions and two read-write data stores. The fundamental limitation with pushdown automata is the inability to look at any arbitrarily selected token in the input stream; it is impossible to examine the surrounding context. If we add an additional stack, it becomes possible to examine all tokens. C is an example of a language that is *Turing complete*. This means that C is able to compute any problem that can be solved by a Turing machine. C can be used to write a lexical analyzer and a parser, but the basic model it represents is far more capable than that of lex or yacc. Similarly, yacc can be used to write lexical analyzers. Yacc's simpler model makes it a better tool for developing parsers than C; similarly, lex's simplicity makes it better for developing lexical analyzers.

In the next chapter, we will begin looking at how to generate the lexical analyzer and parser from specifications that are processed by lex and yacc.

NOTE

For further reading on the theory and practice of compiler design, see the "dragon" book, formally known as *Compilers: Principles, Techniques, and Tools*, by Alfred V. Aho, Ravi Sethi, and Jeffrey D. Ullman, Addison-Wesley, 1988.

2

The Mechanics of Lex and Yacc

Using Lex
Writing a Lex Specification
Using Yacc
Writing a Yacc Specification

In this chapter, we demonstrate the basic operations of lex and yacc. The goal is to help you understand *how* these programs work, what you as a programmer must supply, and what the programs generate. In addition, we show you in more detail than in the previous chapter how the lexical and parsing routines work together.

This chapter covers basic material on lex and yacc. The examples in this chapter are quite simple. Some readers may wish to start at a faster pace, tackling the more complex examples found in Chapter 3, *Building a Calculator*. Nonetheless, you should be sure that you have the basics under your belt before doing so.

Using Lex

There are three steps in using lex:

1. Write a lex specification that matches sequences of characters in the input stream. This file, by convention, has a *.l* suffix.

2. Run lex on the specification. This step generates a file named *lex.yy.c*.

3. Compile *lex.yy.c* and any related source files.

The *lex.yy.c* file that lex generates is not a complete program. It contains a lexical analysis routine called **yylex**. You can either supply a hand-coded **main** routine that calls **yylex** or integrate the lexical analyzer with a yacc-generated parser (which assumes the existence of a lexical analyzer called **yylex**). A lex program also assumes the existence of other support routines. You can supply these routines yourself, or you can use the routines in the UNIX standard library *libl.a*. By linking this library to lex-generated code, you can create a self-standing program.

Writing a Lex Specification

The main section of a lex specification contains a set of rules. The minimum lex specification has the following format:

> %%
> *rules*

%% is required to indicate the start of the rules section in the specification. (There are other sections that we will discuss later.) The specification is created in a file with a suffix of *.l*. This is a useful convention to follow, but it is not required.

Each rule consists of a *regular expression* that is matched against the input stream, and it is associated with an *action* that is performed when a match is made.

We introduced regular expressions for pattern matching in the previous chapter. Regular expressions can make use of a set of *metacharacters* that have special meaning for pattern matching. All other characters are interpreted literally. An expression can be put in quotes, but quotes are required only when the expression contains a blank or a metacharacter that should be interpreted as a literal character. A backslash (\) can also be used to escape any metacharacter.

Actions consist of one or more C language statements.* If more than one state-ment is specified, they must be placed within braces ({ }).

Here is an example of a specification with a single rule:

```
%%
zippy               printf("I recognize zippy");
```

"zippy" is a regular expression in which each character is interpreted literally.

The action that is specified in this example uses **printf**, a C library function. This lex specification states that if "zippy" is recognized in the input stream, then "I recognize zippy" is printed. Any other input will be passed through as is, because it does not match a rule.

Creating Simple Input Scanners

Let's follow these steps in creating several lex-generated input scanners. These programs are not truly lexical analyzers in that they do not return any tokens. They simply scan the input stream and execute a set of actions. Once we have built several of these scanners to understand how lex operates, then we will dis-cuss how to write the specification for a lexical analyzer.

The single-rule lex specification shown previously is in a file named *sample.l*. Let's run lex and process the specification file:

```
$ cat sample.l
%%
zippy               printf("I recognize zippy");
$ lex sample.l
$ ls
lex.yy.c  sample.l
```

lex.yy.c is the C source generated by lex. The next step is to compile the program. However, as we said earlier, *lex.yy.c* is not a complete program. We must link the UNIX standard library *libl.a* by specifying the **-ll** option during compilation:

```
$ cc -o sample lex.yy.c -ll
$ ls
lex.yy.c    sample*      sample.l
```

---

*Technically, an action can be written in the *host* language, which could be RATFOR, a dialect of FORTRAN. The default host language is C, and we will assume that throughout this book.

This command compiles the file *lex.yy.c*, links the object with the library *libl.a*, and creates an executable object file named *sample*. We can test our lex-generated program on a test input file, such as the following one:

```
$ cat test
tom
zippy
harry
zippy and zip
```

A lex-generated program contains a default input routine that takes input from standard input. Therefore, we can use **cat** to pipe the test file to the program, we can use the redirect standard input from a file, or we could type input after executing the command. The following example demonstrates piping the input file to the program:

```
$ cat test | sample
tom
I recognize zippy
harry
I recognize zippy and zip
```

Obviously, this is a rather silly example. Nonetheless, it strips lex down to bare bones and makes it easy to see what is going on.

Now let's look at multiple rule sets. For instance, look at the following set of rules:

```
%%
zip             printf("ZIP");i
zippy           printf("I recognize zippy");
zippy$          printf("I found zippy at the end of the line");
```

The first rule looks for the string "zip" and outputs these letters in caps. The second rule is unchanged from the first example. The third rule looks for the string "zippy" at the end of the line. The metacharacter "$" indicates that a newline must follow the string.* Given multiple rules, lex will match only the rule that produces the longest match. If two rules match the same set of characters, the rule specified first will be applied. If we compile this specification and run it on our test file, it produces the following results:

```
tom
I found zippy at the end of the line
harry
I recognize zippy and ZIP
```

---

*Note that "$" does not match the newline character itself, however.

Notice that a rule matches the longest string possible. The other rules are not matched if a more complete match is made by another rule. For example, "zip", although a substring of "zippy", does not match it because one of the other rules matches it.

The characters that did not match any rule are passed through as is. There is a default rule that echoes the input when the input does not match a specified rule. Therefore, if we want to restrict the output, we have to write explicit rules that match the input and discard it. Look at the following rule:

The dot (.) is a metacharacter that matches any character. The semicolon (;) indicates a null statement in C. Therefore, this rule matches each character in the input that is not otherwise matched, and the null statement causes lex to swallow it. The dot metacharacter does not match a newline, however. So we must write a similar rule to discard the newline:

```
\n    ;
```

The C escape sequence "\n" represents a newline and must be used to match a newline in an expression. The escape sequence "\t" represents a tab, although you can use the TAB key to insert the tab character instead.

The two previous rules could be merged such that each shares the same action. The vertical bar (|) indicates that the action that follows for the next rule applies to the current rule as well:

```
.     |
\n    ;
```

Now let's look at the new specification:

```
%%
zippy           printf("I recognize zippy\n");
.     |
\n    ;
```

Notice that we added a newline to our **printf** statement to compensate for discarding newlines in the last rule. When the program that this specification produces is compiled and run on our sample file, it will output the only line: "I recognize zippy".

Let's do one more variation on this sample program. Let's match more than one name and use the same action for both of them. As in the previous example, we can use the vertical bar to specify that a rule relies upon the action in a subsequent rule. What is different about this one is that we must print the name without knowing which name we have matched. This is possible because lex declares an external character array named **yytext** that contains the string that is matched.

Notice that in the following example, we use the **printf** function to retrieve the value of **yytext**:

```
%%
harry      |
zippy               printf("I recognize %s\n", yytext);
.          |
\n     ;
```

After compiling this specification and running it on our sample file, the program produces the following output:

```
I recognize zippy
I recognize harry
I recognize zippy
```

Using **yytext** is especially important as we use regular expressions to identify patterns in the input. For instance, if we wanted to process strings made up of capital letters, then we could write the following regular expression:

```
[A-Z]+[ \t\n]
```

This regular expression has three elements. Rather than specifying a specific character, we specify a class or range of characters inside brackets ([]). The first part specifies a range of capital letters ([A-Z]). The metacharacter "+" modifies the character class, specifying that we want to match one or more occurrences of capital letters. The last part specifies a range of characters to follow a string of capital letters: a blank space, a tab, or a newline. Here is the regular expression in a lex specification:

```
%%
[A-Z]+[ \t\n]           printf("%s", yytext);
.          ;
```

Whatever the regular expression matches is available in **yytext** and will be printed. All other characters will be ignored.

If our lex specification is named *caps.l*, we can process it with lex and compile the source code, creating a program named **caps**.

Let's see how it works on a test file. First, we'll look at the file and then use the input redirection symbol to supply the input to our program:

```
$ cat test.caps
XView is an API running under the X Window System
that supports the OPEN LOOK GUI.
$ caps < test.caps
API X
OPEN LOOK
```

As you can see, only the capital letters are recognized. The word "GUI" is not recognized, because it is followed by a period rather than a space, a tab, or a newline.

The **ECHO** macro is a useful shorthand for the action of printing what you have matched. We can use it to rewrite the all caps rule as follows:

```
[A-Z]+[ \t\n]        ECHO;
```

The **ECHO** macro is one of several macros defined in *lex.yy.c*.

Scanning Tab-separated Fields

Our next example recognizes tab-separated fields on a line and keeps a count of the current field number. It describes an action to delete the second field from the input. The lex specification follows:

```
%%
        int field_count = 1;
\t      ++field_count;
\n      { ECHO; field_count = 1; }
[^\t\n]+ { if (field_count == 2)
                ;
            else
                printf("%s ", yytext);
        }
```

We begin by declaring and initializing a variable to keep the count of the number of fields on each line. Thus, the **field_count** variable is initialized to 1, and the rule that matches a tab has an action that increments this counter by 1. This is the first example of our placing C code in the lex specification. Lex will add this declaration to local declarations for the function that processes the actions. We'll talk more about including code later on in the chapter.

The next rule looks for a newline, and its action resets the field counter to 1. It also echoes the newline to the output. Notice that this action consists of two statements and that the entire action is placed inside braces ({ }).

The third rule defines a match for the contents of a field. It specifies a character class, using the complementation operator (^) to signify that *all* characters are to be matched *except* those specified in the brackets ([]). In this case, it matches any character except tab or newline; the "+" operator expands the expression to "one or more" occurrences of those characters. Thus, any sequence of characters up to but not including a tab or newline is recognized as a field. The action for the third rule is the most complex one we have seen so far. It uses an **if/else** construct to test the value of the field counter, and if the counter is 2, the action does nothing, meaning that no output is generated. If it is not 2, the **else** clause is executed, and the field is printed.

Let's see an example:

```
$ cat test.cuts
abc        def        ghi        jkl
mno        pqr        stu
wxy        z
$ cat test.cuts | cuts
abc ghi jkl
mno stu
wxy
$
```

This program works, but it is not generalized to work on any field. We can make the program a lot more useful by allowing the user to specify the field number as an argument on the command line. To do that, we need to write our own **main** routine that checks that the number of arguments (**argc**) is at least two (the name of the program and the first parameter) and then uses the value of the first parameter (**argv[1]**) to set a variable named **field_cut**. This **main** routine will be used instead of the one in the library, and it will call **yylex**. *cutter.c* contains our **main** routine:

```
$ cat cutter.c
int field_cut;

main(argc, argv)
int argc;
char *argv[];
{
if (argc > 1)
     field_cut = atoi(argv[1]);
else
     field_cut = 1;
yylex();
}
```

First, we declare **field_cut** to be a global variable. Then the **main** routine follows. It is very simple, testing for the number of arguments and setting the value of **field_cut** to the value of the first parameter, which is the second element in **argv**. If this parameter is not supplied, it defines **field_cut** to be 1. After setting the value of **field_cut**, we call **yylex**.

Now let's look at the new lex specification:

```
$ cat cutter.l
%%
            int field_count = 1;
            extern int field_cut;
\t          ++field_count;
\n          { ECHO; field_count = 1; }
[^\t\n]+    { if (field_count == field_cut)
                ;
            else
                printf("%s ", yytext);
            }
```

The specification is mostly unchanged from the previous example. The only change is that we use the variable **field_cut** instead of the constant 2. This variable, which is defined in the **main** routine in *cutter.c*, is declared as an external variable. The **if** statement now tests **field_count** against the value of **field_cut**.

To compile this specification, we need to specify *cutter.c* on the command line:

```
$ lex cutter.l
$ cc -o cutter cutter.c lex.yy.c -ll
cutter.c:
lex.yy.c:
%
```

Notice that we still have to link in the lex library, because there are other supporting routines that we are not supplying. (These routines are **yywrap** and **yyreject** and are seldom redefined.)

Here are some sample runs that proves our program works:

```
$ cutter 3 < test.cuts
abc def jkl
mno pqr
wxy z
$ cutter < test.cuts
def ghi jkl
pqr stu
z
$
```

Using the Full Specification

In all of our examples so far, we have written specifications that used only the rules section. A full lex specification has three sections, as follows:

> *definitions*
> *%%*
> *rules*
> *%%*
> *user routines*

In the definitions section, you can define simple macros for use in rules. We'll discuss definitions in the next chapter and show other uses of this section in Chapter 6, *A Reference for Lex Specifications*. The rules section is found between the opening *%%* and the closing *%%*. The third section contains C source code that is copied into *lex.yy.c*.

Although having a separate program file is more common, you can include all of the code that we have in *cutter.c* in the lex specification itself. As you can see, we place the **main** routine in the third section. Here is the entire specification:

```
%%
                int field_count = 1;
                extern int field_cut;
\t              ++field_count;
\n              { ECHO;field_count = 1; }
[^\t\n]+        { if (field_count == field_cut)
                      ;
                else
                      printf("%s ", yytext);
                }

%%
int field_cut;

main(argc, argv)
int argc;
char *argv[];
{
if (argc > 1)
      field_cut = atoi(argv[1]);
else
      field_cut = 1;
yylex();
}
```

This file can be processed by lex, and the resulting *lex.yy.c* file can be compiled and linked with the lex library, because all the code is contained in a single file. Once it is compiled, it works as shown in the previous example.

You might want to look at *lex.yy.c* and confirm that it indeed contains C source, although it is not terribly well formatted for reading. Here is a portion of the *lex.yy.c* file generated by the lex specification in *cuts.l*:

```
# include "stdio.h"
.
.
.
int field_cut;
# define YYNEWLINE 10
yylex(){
int nstr; extern int yyprevious;
int field_count = 1;
while((nstr = yylook()) >= 0)
yyfussy: switch(nstr){
case 0:
if(yywrap()) return(0); break;
case 1:
        ++field_count;
break;
case 2:
{ ECHO;field_count = 1; }
break;
case 3:
{ if (field_count == field_cut)
                ;
        else
                printf("%s ", yytext);
        }
break;
case -1:
break;
default:
fprintf(yyout,"bad switch yylook %d",nstr);
} return(0); }
/* end of yylex */
main(argc, argv)
int argc;
char *argv[];
{
if (argc > 1)
     field_cut = atoi(argv[1]);
else
     field_cut = 1;
yylex();
}
.
.
.
```

This portion shows the **yylex** routine that processes the actions. **yylex** consists of a **switch** statement with a case for each rule. Look for the declaration of

field_cut in **yylex**. Also, notice that the user-supplied **main** routine is copied right into the file as is.

Writing a Lexical Analyzer

Now let's look at writing a simple lexical analyzer. The lexical analyzer will be called by the parser each time a new token is needed. In the next section, we look at using yacc to generate that parser.

Our specification will contain regular expressions that match tokens, and our actions will use the **return** statement to communicate with the parser. The lexical analyzer might pass either or both of the following things to the parser:

- A symbol identifying the token.
- The value of the token.

The symbols that identify tokens are defined by the yacc parser. The parser also sets up an external variable **yylval** for the lexical analyzer to pass the value of the token. In addition, a literal character can be passed to the parser as a token whose value is its ASCII value.

Look at the following lex specification:

```
%%
[0-9]+              {
                    sscanf(yytext, "%d", &yylval);
                    return (INTEGER);
                    }
\n                  return ('\n');
```

The rules section contains two rules. The first one matches an integer, defined to be one or more digits. The action associated with this rule passes the value of the token and an identifier for the token. The token matched by lex is available in **yytext**, which is a character array. We use the **sscanf** function to convert this value to a decimal and assign it to the variable **yylval** of type *int*. (In the next chapter, we'll see how to pass token values using multiple data types.) The **return** statement passes the symbol **INTEGER**. The second rule matches the newline, and its corresponding action returns that character.

We can run lex on this specification, but we cannot compile it successfully unless lex has access to the names of tokens, as defined by yacc. There are two ways to access these symbols. One way is to include the lex-generated source file *lex.yy.c* in the yacc specification. We'll see examples of this method in the next section on yacc. The second way is to have yacc generate a header file (*y.tab.h*) and then include that file in the lex specification.

We will demonstrate this method of accessing the parser's symbol definitions in the next chapter.

Using Yacc

Now let's look at using yacc to generate the parser. There are four steps to creating a parser:

1. Write a yacc specification that describes the grammar. This file uses the extension *.y* by convention.

2. Write a lexical analyzer that can produce a token stream. This routine can be generated by lex or hand-coded in C. The name of the lexical routine is **yylex**.

3. Run yacc on the specification to generate the source file for the parser. The output file is named *y.tab.c* for yacc; *bison* uses the filename of the yacc specification (minus the extension) and appends *.tab.c* to it.

4. Compile and link the source files for the parser and the lexical analyzer and any related program files.

The output file *y.tab.c* contains a parsing routine named **yyparse** that calls the lexical routine **yylex** each time a token is needed. Like lex, yacc does not generate a complete program; **yyparse** must be called from a **main** routine. A complete program also requires an error routine named **yyerror** that is called when **yyparse** encounters an error. Both the **main** routine and **yyerror** can be supplied by the programmer, although default versions of these routines are found in the yacc library *liby.a*, and this library can be linked to the parser using the **-ly** option during compilation.

Writing a Yacc Specification

A yacc specification describes a context-free grammar that can be used to generate a parser. This grammar has four classes of elements:*

---

*Based on a description of a context-free grammar in *Compilers: Principles, Techniques, and Tools*, by Alfred V. Aho, Ravi Sethi, and Jeffrey D. Ullman, Addison-Wesley, 1988.

1. Tokens, which are a set of terminal symbols.
2. Syntactical elements, which are a set of nonterminal symbols.
3. Production rules that define a nonterminal symbol (the left-hand side) in terms of a sequence of nonterminals and terminals (the right-hand side).
4. A **start** rule that reduces all the elements of the grammar to a single rule.

The focus of a yacc specification is a set of production rules of the following form:

> *symbol*:   *definition*
> *{action}*
> ;

A colon (:) separates the left-hand from the right-hand side of the rule, and a semicolon (;) terminates the rule. By convention, the definition follows two tab stops after the colon. Also for readability, the semicolon is placed on a line by itself.

Each rule in the grammar is named by a symbol, a nonterminal. The definition consists of zero or more terminal names, such as tokens or literal characters, and other nonterminal symbols. Tokens, which are terminal symbols recognized by the lexical analyzer, are permitted only on the right-hand side of a rule. Each definition can have an action written in C associated with it. This action is placed inside braces ({ }). We will talk more about actions later on.

Rules that share the same left-hand side can be combined using a vertical bar (|). This allows alternate definitions within a rule. The semicolon is not necessary at the end of a rule when it is followed by a vertical bar.

The name of a symbol can be any length, consisting of letters, dot (.), underscore (_), and digits (anywhere except in first position). Upper-case and lower-case character sets are distinct. The names of nonterminal symbols are lower case by convention, while token names are capitalized.

If input does not conform to the grammar, then the parser will print the message "syntax error." This message is output by the default **yyerror** routine, which can be redefined by the programmer to provide more information. An example of redefining **yyerror** is shown in Chapter 4, *The MGL.*

A minimal yacc specification consists of a rules section preceded by a declaration of the tokens used in the grammar.

The full format of a yacc specification has the following elements:

declarations
%%
grammar rules
%%
C programs

The format of the specification is very similar to lex. The declarations section contains information that affects the operation of yacc. The declarations section makes use of several keywords to define tokens and their characteristics. Each of these keywords is followed by a list of tokens or quoted literal characters.

%token	Declare the names of tokens.
%left	Define left-associative operators.
%right	Define right-associative operators.
%nonassoc	Define operators that may not associate with themselves.
%type	Declare the type of nonterminals.
%union	Declare multiple data types for semantic values.
%start	Declare the start symbol. Default is first in rules section.
%prec	Assign precedence to a rule.

There is also another set of declarations that affect the operation of yacc, and they are discussed in Chapter 7, *A Reference for Yacc Specifications*.

The declarations section can also contain C code to declare variables or types as well as to define macros. It can also contain **#include** statements to include header files. This is done the same way in yacc as it is in lex:

%{
C declarations
%}

Anything between %{ and %} is copied directly to the file generated by yacc.

The rules section contains the production rules that describe the grammar. The C programs section is optional, but it can contain any user-supplied C code. It might specify the lexical analyzer routine **yylex**, a **main** routine, or subroutines used by actions in the rules section.

Comments, appearing as they are in C (/* ... */), can be placed anywhere that a symbol name can appear. Blanks, tabs, and newlines are ignored in the specification.

Let's look at a simple grammar built around a single token: **INTEGER**. The function of this specification is to generate a program that prints any number it receives as input:

```
$ cat print-int.y
%token INTEGER

%%

lines:    /* empty */
     | lines line
     { printf("= %d\n", $2 ); }
     ;

line:     INTEGER '\n'
     { $$ = $1; }
     ;
%%
#include "lex.yy.c"
```

In the declarations section, we declare the token **INTEGER**. This will translate into a **#define** statement that associates a numeric constant with this symbol. This symbol is used for communication between the lexical analyzer and the parser. We will come back to this line later when we discuss writing the lexical analyzer.

In the rules section, we specify a grammar made up of two groupings: **lines** and **line**. The first rule defines **lines** to be zero or more lines of input. The first of the two alternate definitions is empty. This is a conventional definition that means the empty string is permissible as input. (That does not mean that blank lines are valid, however.) The second alternate definition is recursive, stating that the input consists of one or more lines. The nonterminal symbol **line** is defined in the second rule. It consists of an **INTEGER** token followed by a newline.

Now let's consider the actions associated with these rules. We said earlier that actions consist of one or more C language statements. Yacc provides additional *pseudo-variables* that make it easier for the actions to get the value of a symbol and set the value returned by the action. The dollar sign symbol ($) has special meaning for yacc. The value of each element of a definition can be retrieved using positional notation: "$1" for the first token, "$2" for the second, and so on. The value returned by the action is set by assigning that value to "$$". Look at the action associated with the **line** rule:

```
line:     INTEGER '\n'
     { $$ = $1; }
```

Thus, this action returns the value of the **INTEGER** token. Note that there are two elements in the definition, but the newline is not returned. The value of the **INTEGER** token is passed to the action associated with the **lines** rule:

```
| lines line
{ printf("= %d\n", $2 );
```

In this action, "$2" refers to the value of **line**.

The third part of our sample yacc specification contains an **#include** statement that includes the source code for the lexical analyzer. Earlier in this chapter, we created a simple lexical analyzer that recognizes the token **INTEGER** and a new-line.

Let's do a test of this specification, assuming that the lex specification is in *print-int.l* and the yacc specification is in *print-int.y*. Here is the series of commands for creating an executable program named **print-int**:

```
$ lex print-int.l
$ yacc print-int.y
$ cc -o print-int y.tab.c -ly -ll
```

The first two commands can be performed in any order as long as both are done before compilation. Because the yacc specification includes the source file for the lexical analyzer, *lex.yy.c* is not specified for compilation. Also, notice that both yacc and lex libraries are specified on the command line for compilation. The order is significant because you want the **main** routine supplied by the yacc library.

Finally, let's take our program out for a test run:

```
$ print-int
3
= 3
15
= 15
6
= 6
zippy
syntax error
$
```

This program reads the input and, if it is a number, prints it, preceded by an equal sign. When the parser encounters a string, it prints the message "syntax error."

A Specification for a Simple Adding Machine

In this section, we build lex and yacc specifications for an "adding machine." This machine keeps a running total and allows us to add or subtract from that total. We can also reset the total to zero or any other number. The input consists of a number optionally preceded by a plus, a minus, or an equal sign. For instance, if the first input is "4" or "+4", "= 4" is printed. If the next input is "-3", then "= 1" is printed. If the input is "=" or "= 0", the total will be reset to 0, and "= 0" is printed.

Let's look at the yacc specification:

```
$ cat addup.y
%{
int sum_total = 0;
%}

%token INTEGER

%%

lines:    /* empty */
      | lines line
      ;

line:      '\n'
      | exp '\n'
      { printf("= %d\n", sum_total); }
      ;

exp:  INTEGER        {sum_total += $1; }
      | '+' INTEGER      {sum_total += $2; }
      | '-' INTEGER      {sum_total -= $2; }
      | '=' INTEGER      {sum_total = $2; }
      | '='              {sum_total = 0; }
      ;

%%
#include "lex.yy.c"
```

The main action in this specification is to set the variable **sum_total** based on the input and then print the new value. The declarations section contains the declaration and initialization of **sum_total**. We create this variable to keep the current total. Next we declare a single token, **INTEGER**.

The first rule of the rules section is mostly unchanged from the previous example. This time, however, there is no action associated with it. You may need to experiment by removing this rule to fully understand why it is needed. It allows our program to read a series of lines, not just a single line.

The rule for **line** has alternate definitions. Either a newline by itself or an **exp** followed by a newline are accepted. Thus, blank lines can be input to the program without causing a syntax error. An **exp** followed by a newline executes the action of printing the current total.

The rule for **exp** also has alternate definitions. An **INTEGER** token, a plus, minus, or equal sign followed by an **INTEGER** token, and an equal sign by itself are accepted. Each action associated with a definition assigns a new value to **sum_total**. Note that we do not assign the new value to "$$", because we need to accumulate this value from one input line to the next.

At the end of the specification, we have included the source file for the lexical analyzer that will be generated by lex.

Writing the Lexical Analyzer

Our adding machine needs a lexical analyzer similar to one we developed earlier in the chapter. We need to improve it to handle "+", "-", and "=". In addition, we will add the ability to exit gracefully from the adding machine.

Here is the lex specification:

```
%%
[0-9]+      {
            sscanf(yytext, "%d", &yylval);
            return (INTEGER);
            }
\n          return ('\n');

[-+=]       return yytext[0];

quit        return 0;
.           ;
```

The rule that recognizes the **INTEGER** token is the same as before. So is the rule that matches the newline. The third rule is new. It specifies matching any of three characters. The action returns the first character of the **yytext** character array. We could have matched each character and returned that character; however, this is a more general method. The next rule matches the string "quit" and returns 0. Returning 0 will cause the parser to quit. Notice that we do not pass the string "quit" to the parser. Also, we could rewrite this pattern to allow a number of different ways to quit:

```
q|(quit)|(exit)|x
```

This regular expression can evaluate four different alternatives, any of which cause lex to return 0. Finally, any character that we have not matched so far is discarded.

Creating the Parser

Now we can generate the lexical analyzer and the parser and compile our program:

```
$ lex addup.l
$ yacc addup.y
$ cc -o addup y.tab.c -ly -ll
```

We link both lex and yacc libraries and use the default support routines. Now we can test the program. After entering the command name, we can begin entering numbers. Each number is added to or subtracted from the accumulated total, and the total is printed. Here is a sample run:

```
$ addup
3
= 3
5
= 8
+4
= 12
-2
= 10
= 0
= 0
4
= 4
250
= 254
= 100
= 100
-50
= 50
quit
$
```

As simple as it is, it does what it is supposed to do.

By now, you should have a good understanding of *how* to use lex and yacc. It is a good idea to play around with these simple examples, adding or removing constructs and experimenting to see what happens. In subsequent chapters, we will be going into examples of increasing complexity, beginning with a full-fledged calculator in the next chapter.

3

Building a Calculator

Nearly everything we have seen written on lex and yacc undertakes the development of a calculator. In this chapter, we contribute to that tradition. One reason for choosing a calculator is that the syntax of a calculator is straightforward, consisting of operators and operands. Another good reason for choosing a calculator is that not a lot of code is needed to implement the semantic actions.

The Calculator as Interpreter

The purpose of this section is to sketch the complementary roles of the lexical analyzer and the parser in developing a calculator. Then we will proceed with developing the actual specifications.

A calculator is one kind of interpreter. When it is given a simple mathematical problem, such as "3 + 4", a result is immediately displayed. Any calculator, to be usable, should provide the basic arithmetic functions: addition, subtraction, multiplication, and division. Recalling the basic model we presented in Figure 1-2, our input comes from the user in the form of numbers and operators. A lex-generated lexical analyzer will be responsible for converting user input into a stream of tokens that yacc must in turn recognize to know what operation to perform. For example, if the user types:

```
36.7 + 43.2
```

our lexical analyzer will match three tokens of the form:

REAL PLUS REAL

Our parser needs to have a rule that recognizes this as a valid numeric equation. For instance, our grammar might have a rule named **rexpr** (for real expression); such a rule, narrowly described here, is shown below written in BNF:

rexpr ← **REAL** | rexpr '+' rexpr

A **rexpr** is made up of a **REAL** token or a **rexpr**, a "+", and then a **rexpr**. The action associated with the first definition simply returns the value of the token, while second definition returns the value of an addition operation:

```
{ $$ = $1 + $3; }
```

Our grammar also requires a rule to recognize an expression followed by a newline.

line ← '\n' | rexpr '\n'

This action for this rule would actually print the result of the operation.

Writing Regular Expressions for Tokens

Our lexical analyzer must be able to recognize the two types of operands that we expect: *integers* and *real numbers*. (A more complex implementation might also include support for complex numbers, vectors, etc.)

For this application, we define a real number as the following sequence: an optional leading unary minus, any sequence of digits, a decimal point followed by any sequence of digits, an optional exponent indicator (**e** or **E**), an optional unary plus or minus, and a sequence of digits which are present if and only if the exponent indicator is present. An integer is a sequence of digits that does not match the definition of a real number. The following are all valid real numbers:

```
3.1415926
2.718281828
6.02E28
```

while these are not:

```
1
3.
2.4E
```

In the above example, the first one *is* a valid integer but neither of the others is.

Using the definitions we just stated, we can now turn our attention to actually producing the regular expressions for our lex specification. We will start with the simplest such pattern—that of an integer:

```
[0-9]+
```

This regular expression means "any sequence of one or more digits." Note that when the lexical analyzer interprets the meaning of this definition, it will *always* take the longest match possible. This prevents a number like:

```
415926
```

from being interpreted as *two* integers, say, 415 and 926. Thus, when scanning the input, the lexical analyzer would detect a single integer.

The regular expression for a real number is a bit more complex but is still similar to the lex definition we used for an integer:

```
([0-9]*"."[0-9]+)|([0-9]*"."[0-9]+[eE][+-]?[0-9]+)
```

This example consists of two parts. The first part:

```
[0-9]*"."[0-9]+
```

represents a real number without an exponent; that is, it consists of zero or more digits, followed by a decimal point, followed by one or more digits. The second part:

```
[0-9]*"."[0-9]+[eE][+-]?[0-9]+
```

represents a real number with an exponent; that is, a sequence of zero or more digits, followed by a decimal point, followed by one or more digits, followed by an "e", either lower or upper case, followed by either a plus, a minus, or a digit, and then finished with zero or more additional digits.

This is not the only way possible to describe a real number; in Chapter 6, *A Reference for Lex Specifications*, we describe the full range of lex's regular expressions.

Defining Substitution Strings

One of the most common uses of the definitions section of a lex specification is to define substitution strings. The syntax for a definition is:

   name   *translation*

name must begin with a letter. It must be separated from *translation* by at least one tab or blank. The name can then be used in a rule as such:

   [*name*]

Definitions are particularly useful in building complex lexical analyzers where regular expressions are constructed from a set of basic parts.

We can specify these regular expressions as a series of definitions that will appear in the definitions section of our lex specification:

```
integer   [0-9]+
dreal     ([0-9]*"."[0-9]+)
ereal     ([0-9]*"."[0-9]+[eE][+-]?[0-9]+)
real      {dreal}|{ereal}
nl        \n
```

Look at how the regular expression for real numbers is broken into two parts, **dreal** and **ereal**, and then combined using the alternation operator. Once defined, substitutions can be used in the definitions section as well as in the rules.

Defining the Token Types

The token number is passed to **yyparse** as the return value of **yylex**. The value of the token is passed through the external variable **yylval**. Before writing the actions for our lex specification, we need to look at how to define different token types in the yacc specification.

The default type of **yylval** is an *int*. The macro **YYSTYPE** is used to define the default data type expected by yacc. If you want to define a data type other than *int*, you can place a #**define** statement in the declarations section of the yacc specification. For instance, if we decided that our calculator needs to support double precision floating point numbers, we would redefine **YYSTYPE** to be **double** as follows:

```
%{
#define YYSTYPE double
%}
```

YYSTYPE is used to set the type for **yylval**.

If there is more than one data type for token values, **yylval** is declared as a **union**, and the token types are associated with each member of the **union**.

Our calculator must accept the tokens **INTEGER** and **REAL**. **INTEGER** is obviously of type *int*, but **REAL** should be of type *double*. The following declaration using the **%union** keyword is placed in the declarations section of our calculator's yacc specification:

```
%union {
    double    real;     /* real value */
    int     integer;    /* integer value */
    }
```

Thus, the tokens consist of one of two possible data types: a "real" (declared as a C *double*) and an "integer" (declared as a C *int*). The **union** declaration could also appear outside the yacc specification in a header file as follows:

```
typedef union {
    double    real;     /* real value */
    int     integer;    /* integer value */
    } YYSTYPE
```

This header file must be specified in an **#include** statement in the declarations section of the yacc specification.

The yacc specification must also associate the name of each union member with the terminal and nonterminal names used in the grammar. The keyword **%token** is used to define the token type. The name of the union member is placed in angle brackets (<>), followed by the token name. Our calculator requires the following token type name declaration:

```
%token <real> REAL
%token <integer> INTEGER
```

The **%type** keyword is used to define the value type of nonterminal symbols that use token values. As you will see shortly, our rules section consists of integer expressions, named **iexpr**, and real expressions, named **rexpr**. The declarations section of our yacc specification defines these names as follows:

```
%type <real> rexpr
%type <integer> iexpr
```

You can use a single **%type** or **%token** statement to declare multiple symbols of the same type.

Multiple data types affect the lex specification because we have redefined **yylval** as a union. Now when we refer to **yylval** to return the value of a token, we must specify which member of the union to use. For instance, to return a **REAL** value to the parser, we write the following action:

```
        { sscanf(yytext,"%lf", &yylval.real);
          return REAL;
        }
```

Similarly, the value of the **INTEGER** token is placed in **yylval.integer**.

Completing the Lex Specification

Now that we know what our token types are, we can complete our lex specification:

```
%{
#include "y.tab.h"
%}
integer    [0-9]+
dreal      ([0-9]*"."[0-9]+)
ereal      ([0-9]*"."[0-9]+[eE][+-]?[0-9]+)
real       {dreal}|{ereal}
nl         \n

%%

[ \t]+      ;
{integer}   { sscanf(yytext,"%d", &yylval.integer);
              return INTEGER;
            }
{real}      { sscanf(yytext,"%lf", &yylval.real);
              return REAL;
            }
{nl}        { extern int lineno;   lineno++;
              return '\n';
            }
.           { return yytext[0]; }
%%
```

In the first section, the C declarations section, we begin by including the yacc-generated header file *y.tab.h*; this provides definitions of the symbols **INTEGER** and **REAL** and the yacc **union** structure. Once we have written the yacc specification, we can generate this header file by specifying the **-d** option when running yacc on the specification.

Next we see our definitions, which we discussed earlier. The %% indicates the end of the lex declarations section and the beginning of the lex rules section.

The first rule matches a blank or a tab; the corresponding action is to do nothing. This is how a symbol is *ignored*. No value is returned, and lexical analysis continues. The second line matches our "integer" pattern, and if the match is an integer, the string is converted, using **sscanf**, into an integer value. This value is made available to the parser as **yylval.integer**. Finally, the value INTEGER, which comes from the *y.tab.h* header file, is returned to the caller of **yylex**.

The third pattern matches our definition of a "real". If a match is made against the pattern, then the resulting string is converted into a REAL and passed to the parser as **yylval.real**. The symbol REAL is also returned.

At this point, you might note that the definition of an integer and the definition of a real conflict, that is, the pattern for an integer, would also match a real number. However, lex does *not* match based upon the order in which the patterns are listed. Rather, lex matches the longest possible pattern. So, if "123.45" is in the buffer, it will *not* match "123" as an integer. It will match "123.45" as a real, because it is the longer match.

Finally, we finish up with an action for a newline, which increments the **lineno** variable and returns the newline that is followed by the default action for any single character match, which merely returns the character itself. This is how characters such as "+", "-", and "*" are passed as literal character values.

Creating the Yacc Specification

Now that we have a lex specification, we need to generate the accompanying yacc grammar. We have already discussed many elements of this specification earlier in the section "Defining the Token Types." Let's look at the declarations section:

```
%{
#include <stdio.h>
%}

%union {
    double    real;      /* real value */
    int       integer;   /* integer value */
}

%token <real> REAL
%token <integer> INTEGER

%type <real> rexpr
%type <integer> iexpr

%left '+' '-'
%left '*' '/'
%left UMINUS
```

First, we define the yacc *union* that contains the data values returned by the **yylex** routine. It defines a collection of two possible data types: a "real" and an "integer". Recall that in the lex actions, we used these fields when converting the data from string form to internal form. Yacc will, in turn, access these data types via this union.

Next we define the two possible token types returned by the lexical analyzer. We use **%token** to define them, so that yacc will generate the appropriate definitions in the header file used by the lexical analyzer. Thus, when **yylex** returns the value **REAL**, the data is contained in **yylval.real**, and when it returns **INTEGER**, the data is contained in **yylval.integer**.

Next we have some declarations for nonterminal names. These rules will be declared in the rules section:

```
%type <real> rexpr
%type <integer> iexpr
```

These statements tell yacc that the rule *rexpr* returns data in the *real* portion of the union and *iexpr* returns data in the *integer* portion of the union.

Finally, we define the *associativity* of the mathematical operators. Here is our sample declaration:

```
%left '+' '-'
%left '*' '/'
%left UMINUS
```

These declarations are stated in order from lowest to highest precedence. The first one declares that "+" and "−" are left-associative and of lowest precedence; "*" and "/" are also left-associative, but they are of higher precedence than "+" and "−". Finally, the list terminates with the pseudo-operator **UMINUS** that will be used for assigning the precedence of the unary minus, which binds more tightly than the binary minus. We will look at associativity and precedence in greater detail in Chapter 7, *A Reference for Yacc Specifications*.

After the yacc declarations come the grammar's production rules. These rules describe the *form* of the grammar, along with the *actions* to take upon recognizing a particular pattern. Like the lex specification, this is done through pattern matching. Unlike the lex specification, the patterns are very flexible.

First, we have a rule that describes all possible operations on integers:

```
iexpr: INTEGER
     | iexpr '+' iexpr
       { $$ = $1 + $3; }
     | iexpr '-' iexpr
       { $$ = $1 - $3; }
     | iexpr '*' iexpr
       { $$ = $1 * $3; }
     | iexpr '/' iexpr
       { if($3) $$ = $1 / $3;
```

```
        else {
          fprintf(stderr,"divide by zero\n");
          yyerror;
        }
      }
    | '-' iexpr %prec UMINUS
      { $$ = - $2; }
    | '(' iexpr ')'
      { $$ = $2; }
    ;
```

An **iexpr** (meaning integer expression) can be any one of the listed items. For example, an **INTEGER** (the token returned by **yylex**) constitutes an **iexpr**. The *action* is the default action: return the *value* of **yylval.integer**. The next possibility is any two **iexpr**'s joined by a "+" sign. In this case, there is an explicit action: return the result of adding the two **iexpr**'s together. Similarly, we have "−" and "*". Unlike the previous examples, "/" must be handled as a special case, simply because division by zero is prohibited. Once the division by zero is checked, the operation is performed. If division by zero *is* attempted, a warning message is printed, and the special instruction **yyerror** is executed. We'll look at what **yyerror** does shortly.

The unary minus rule uses the **%prec** keyword to tell yacc that this rule binds with the specified precedence (in this case, **UMINUS**). The final rule is that any **iexpr** may be enclosed by parentheses, (). The rules for the **rexpr** are similar, although they contain additional cases to allow conversions between integers and reals:

```
rexpr:  REAL
    | rexpr '+' rexpr
            { $$ = $1 + $3; }
    | rexpr '-' rexpr
            { $$ = $1 - $3; }
    | rexpr '*' rexpr
            { $$ = $1 * $3; }
    | rexpr '/' rexpr
            { if($3) $$ = $1 / $3;
              else {
                fprintf(stderr,"divide by zero\n");
                yyerror;
              }
            }
    | '-' rexpr %prec UMINUS
            { $$ = - $2; }
    | '(' rexpr ')'
            { $$ = $2; }
    | iexpr '+' rexpr
            { $$ = (double)$1 + $3; }
    | iexpr '-' rexpr
            { $$ = (double)$1 - $3; }
```

```
      | iexpr '*' rexpr
                { $$ = (double)$1 * $3; }
      | iexpr '/' rexpr
                { if($3) $$ = (double)$1 / $3;
                  else {
                      fprintf(stderr,"divide by zero\n");
                      yyerror;
                  }
                }
      | rexpr '+' iexpr
                { $$ = $1 + (double)$3; }
      | rexpr '-' iexpr
                { $$ = $1 - (double)$3; }
      | rexpr '*' iexpr
                { $$ = $1 * (double)$3; }
      | rexpr '/' iexpr
                { if($3) $$ = $1 / (double)$3;
                  else {
                      fprintf(stderr,"divide by zero\n");
                      yyerror;
                  }
                }
      ;
```

The rules section ends with the (now familiar) %%, which also signals the beginning of the code section. This section contains two simple routines:

```
char *progname;
int lineno;

main(argc,argv)
int argc;
char **argv;
{
    progname = argv[0];

    yyparse();
}

yyerror(s) /* print warning message */
char *s;
{
    fprintf(stderr, "%s: %s", progname, s);
    fprintf(stderr, " line %d\n", lineno);
}
```

The external variable **progname** merely points to the program name from the argument list, while the **lineno** variable is used for keeping track of the current line number. The routine **main** sets the **progname** variable and then simply calls **yyparse**; note that the yacc library version simply calls **yyparse**. The **yyerror** routine prints the program name, the error message, and then the line number of the suspected error.

Our final yacc grammar file is shown in Example 3-1.

Example 3-1. Calculator's yacc grammar

```
%{
#include <stdio.h>
%}

%union {
    double     real;     /* real value */
    int      integer;     /* integer value */
}

%token <real> REAL
%token <integer> INTEGER

%type <real> rexpr
%type <integer> iexpr

%left '+' '-'
%left '*' '/'
%left UMINUS

%%

lines:   /* nothing */
       | lines line
       ;

line:    '\n'
       | iexpr '\n'
               { printf("%d\n",$1); }
       | rexpr '\n'
               { printf("%15.8lf\n",$1); }
       | error '\n'
               { yyerror; }
       ;

iexpr:   INTEGER
       | iexpr '+' iexpr
               { $$ = $1 + $3; }
       | iexpr '-' iexpr
               { $$ = $1 - $3; }
       | iexpr '*' iexpr
               { $$ = $1 * $3; }
       | iexpr '/' iexpr
               { if($3) $$ = $1 / $3;
                 else {
                    fprintf(stderr,"divide by zero\n");
                    yyerror;
                 }
               }
       | '-' iexpr %prec UMINUS
```

Example 3-1. Calculator's yacc grammar (continued)

```
                    { $$ = - $2; }
        |   '(' iexpr ')'
                    { $$ = $2; }
        ;

rexpr:    REAL
        | rexpr '+' rexpr
                { $$ = $1 + $3; }
        | rexpr '-' rexpr
                { $$ = $1 - $3; }
        | rexpr '*' rexpr
                { $$ = $1 * $3; }
        | rexpr '/' rexpr
                { if($3) $$ = $1 / $3;
                    else {
                        fprintf(stderr,"divide by zero\n");
                        yyerror;
                    }
                }
        | '-' rexpr %prec UMINUS
                { $$ = - $2; }
        |   '(' rexpr ')'
                { $$ = $2; }
        | iexpr '+' rexpr
                { $$ = (double)$1 + $3; }
        | iexpr '-' rexpr
                { $$ = (double)$1 - $3; }
        | iexpr '*' rexpr
                { $$ = (double)$1 * $3; }
        | iexpr '/' rexpr
                { if($3) $$ = (double)$1 / $3;
                    else {
                        fprintf(stderr,"divide by zero\n");
                        yyerror;
                    }
                }
        | rexpr '+' iexpr
                { $$ = $1 + (double)$3; }
        | rexpr '-' iexpr
                { $$ = $1 - (double)$3; }
        | rexpr '*' iexpr
                { $$ = $1 * (double)$3; }
        | rexpr '/' iexpr
                { if($3) $$ = $1 / (double)$3;
                    else {
                        fprintf(stderr,"divide by zero\n");
                        yyerror;
                    }
                }
        ;
%%
```

Example 3-1. Calculator's yacc grammar (continued)

```
char *progname;
int lineno;

main(argc,argv)
int argc;
char **argv;
{
    progname = argv[0];

    yyparse();
}

yyerror(s) /* print warning message */
char *s;
{
    fprintf(stderr, "%s: %s", progname, s);
    fprintf(stderr, " line %d\n", lineno);
}
```

Compilation

Now that we actually have the lex and yacc specifications for our sample calculator, we can create a working program from it.

If *calc.l* is the name of the sample lex file, you enter the following command to create the C code:

```
$ lex calc.l
```

If *calc.y* is the yacc grammar and *calc.l* is the lex specification, then we compile *calc* as follows:

```
$ lex calc.l
$ yacc -d calc.y
```

The **-d** option to yacc produces the header file *y.tab.h*, which we have included in the lex specification.

The following line compiles the output generated by lex and yacc and creates our program:

```
$ cc -o calc y.tab.c lex.yy.c -ly -ll
```

Because our yacc specification supplied the **main** and **yyerror** routines, linking the yacc library here is not really necessary. The first **main** routine encountered will be the one used.

Showing the Results

Now that we have successfully built the calculator, we take it for a test run.

```
% calc
23 * 34
782
14 + 5
19
12 * 23.3
    279.60000000
1 / 0
divide by zero
1
1 + 0
1
2.3 * 3.2
      7.36000000
3.14 * 45
    141.30000000
255 * 255
65025
255 * 255 + ( 3.2 * 4.3)
  65038.76000000
1024 * 1024
1048576
%
```

Although this calculator is a simple example of how lex and yacc can be used, it provides the basis from which a full-scale calculation language can be derived. It also fully demonstrates how very useful lex and yacc can be—this sample would have taken significantly longer had it been written by hand in C.

Lex and Yacc in Makefiles

The process of compilation can be aided by custom shell scripts or by the use of makefiles. In this section, we take a brief look at support that the **make** utility provides for lex and yacc.

Just as **make** understands how to build *.o* files from *.c* files or *.s* files, it also understands how to make *.o* files from *.l* or *.y* files. For example, if the current directory contains the file *calc.l* and we wish to make *sample.o* from this file, the following suffices:

```
% make calc.o
lex   calc.l
cc   -c lex.yy.c
mv lex.yy.o sample.o
%
```

make includes a number of built-in macros to describe both lex and yacc. They can, of course, be used as is or modified to use GNU *bison* or *flex* (discussed in Appendices C and D). The list in Table 3-1 describes the internal **make** macros relating to lex and yacc.

Table 3-1: make Internal Macros

Macro	Description	Default Contents
LEX	Name of "lex" program	lex
LFLAGS	Flags to pass to lex	empty
YACC	Name of "yacc" program	yacc
YFLAGS	Flags to pass to yacc	empty

Other macros may be provided for different versions of yacc.*

For a project of any size, makefiles are essential. While working on the calculator project, we developed a simple makefile you will find useful for future work; it is shown in Example 3-2.

---

*One system we used included YACCR, which supposedly invoked RATFOR yacc, a variant no longer supported.

Example 3-2. Calculator's sample makefile

```
YFLAGS=-d
LIBS=-ll

calc: lex.o calc.o
      cc -o $@ $? $(LIBS)

lex.o: y.tab.h

y.tab.h: calc.c
```

4

The MGL

Overview of the MGL
Developing the MGL
Building the MGL
Screen Processing
Termination
Sample MGL Code

In the previous chapter, we provided a simple example of an interpreter, the desktop calculator. In this chapter, we turn our attention to compiler design by developing a *menu generation language* (*MGL*) and its associated compiler. We begin with a full description of the language that we are going to create. Then we look at several iterations of developing the lex and yacc specifications. Lastly, we create the actions associated with our grammar and which implement the features of the MGL.

Overview of the MGL

We are going to develop a language that can be used to generate a custom menu interface. It will take as input a description file and produce a C program that can be compiled to create this output on a user's terminal. The menu description consists of the following:

1. A screen and a name.

2. A title (or titles).

3. A list of:

   items, [command], actions, and [attributes]

   where *item* is the text string that appears on the menu, *command* is the mnemonic used to provide command line access to the functions of the menu system, *action* is the procedure that should be performed when a menu item is chosen, and *attribute* indicates how this item should be handled.

4. A terminator.

5. Additional menus.

A sample menu description file is:

```
screen myMenu
title "My First Menu"
title "by Tony Mason"
item "List Things to Do"
command "to-do"
action execute list-things-todo
attribute command
item "Quit"
command "quit"
action quit
end myMenu
```

This description is processed by the MGL compiler and produces C code, which must itself be compiled. When the resulting program is executed, it creates the following menu:

```
      My First Menu
      by Tony Mason

1) List Things to Do
2) Quit
```

When the user selects item 1 or enters the command "to-do", then the procedure "list-things-todo" is executed.

A more general description of this format is:

```
screen <name>
title <string>
item <string>
command <string>
action <execute,menu,quit,ignore> <name>
attribute <visible,invisible>
end <name>
```

Now as we turn to developing this language, we will start with a small amount of this functionality and add to it over several iterations to implement the full specification as described here. One advantage of this approach is to show you how easy it is to modify the lex-generated lexical analyzer and the yacc-generated parser as changes are made in the language.

Developing the MGL

Menus are commonly used to provide a simple, clean interface for inexperienced users. For these users, the rigidity and ease of use provided by a menu system is ideal.

One major disadvantage to menus is that they inhibit experienced users from moving directly into the particular desired application. For these people, a command-driven interface is more desirable. However, all but the most experienced users might occasionally want to fall back into the menu to access some seldom used function.

Our MGL should be designed with both these design constraints in mind. Initially, then, suppose we start with two keywords:

- **choice**

- **command**

where **choice** indicates a choice that can be made by the menu user, while **command** indicates a command that can be issued by a more experienced user to access some particular function.

This is a start but hardly constitutes a usable language. Nevertheless, we can sketch out a lexical specification for this "language":

```
ws          [ \t]+
nl          \n
%%
{ws}        ;
choice      { yylval.cmd = CHOICE;
              return yylval.cmd; }
command     { yylval.cmd = COMMAND;
              return yylval.cmd; }
{nl}        { lineno++; }
.           { return yytext[0];}
```

and its corresponding yacc grammar:

```
%{
#include <stdio.h>
%}

%union {
        int cmd;          /* command value */
        int nothing;      /* filler */
}

%token <cmd> CHOICE COMMAND
%%
start:   CHOICE
       | COMMAND
       ;
```

Our lexical analyzer is very simple in that it looks for our keywords and returns the appropriate token when it recognizes one. If the parser sees either token **CHOICE** or **COMMAND**, then the **start** rule will be fulfilled, and **yyparse** will return successfully.

Each item on a menu should have an *action* associated with it. We can introduce the keyword **action**. One action might be to *ignore* the entry, and another might be to *execute* a program; we can add the keywords **ignore** and **execute**.

Thus, a sample entry using our modified vocabulary might be:

```
choice action execute
```

We must be able to tell it *what* to execute, so we add our first noncommand argument, a string. Because program names could contain punctuation, etc., we will presume that a program name is a *quoted string*. Now our sample entry becomes:

```
choice action execute "/bin/sh"
```

We can modify our lex specification to support the new keywords, as well as the new token type. It then becomes:

```
ws          [ \t]+
qstring     \"[^\"\n]*[\"\n]
nl          \n
%%
{ws}        ;
{qstring}   { yylval.string = yytext;
              return yylval.cmd; }
action      { yylval.cmd = ACTION;
              return yylval.cmd; }
execute     { yylval.cmd = EXECUTE;
              return yylval.cmd; }
choice      { yylval.cmd = CHOICE;
              return yylval.cmd; }
```

```
command     { yylval.cmd = COMMAND;
              return yylval.cmd; }
ignore      { yylval.cmd = IGNORE;
              return yylval.cmd; }
{nl}        { lineno++; }
.           { return yytext[0]; }
```

Note our complex definition of a quoted string. This is necessary to prevent lex from matching a line like:

```
"apples" and "oranges"
```

as a single token. This is accomplished by the `[^\"\n]*` part of the pattern, which says match against every character that is not a quotation mark or a new-line. We do not want to match beyond a newline because a missing closing quo-tation mark can cause the lexical analyzer to wrap through as many lines as nec-essary to match. This can easily cause an overflow of internal buffers, which are typically of limited size, an event that would lead to a rather unfriendly user error:

```
$ froboz myfile Bus error--core dumped
```

At least with this method, we will be able to report the error condition to the user in a more polite manner.

Now we also need to modify our yacc grammar:

```
%{
#include <stdio.h>
%}

%union {
        int cmd;                /* command value */
        char *string;           /* string buffer */
}

%token <cmd> CHOICE COMMAND ACTION IGNORE EXECUTE
%token <string> QSTRING
%%
start:   CHOICE action
       | COMMAND action
       ;

action:  ACTION IGNORE
       | ACTION EXECUTE QSTRING
       ;
%%
```

Note that we added a type to the union, the "string" type, and that we now have a new token, **QSTRING**, which represents a quoted string.

After looking at our briefly sketched model, it seems the distinction between a choice and a command might not be necessary. Perhaps, instead, it is possible to simply provide a single short command for *each* choice if so desired. Now we will introduce each such new entry as an *item*, by using the keyword **item**. If there is a command associated, we will indicate that by using the **command** keyword. Our lex specification then becomes:

```
ws          [ \t]+
qstring     \"[^\"\n]*[\"\n]
nl          \n
%%
{ws}        ;
{qstring}   { yylval.string = yytext;
              return QSTRING; }
action      { yylval.cmd = ACTION;
              return yylval.cmd; }
execute     { yylval.cmd = EXECUTE;
              return yylval.cmd; }
command     { yylval.cmd = COMMAND;
              return yylval.cmd; }
ignore      { yylval.cmd = IGNORE;
              return yylval.cmd; }
item        { yylval.cmd = ITEM;
              return yylval.cmd; }
{nl}        { lineno++; }
.           { return yytext[0]; }
```

Although we have changed the fundamental structure of the language, there is little change in the lexical analyzer. Rather, much of the change shows up in the yacc grammar:

```
%{
#include <stdio.h>
%}

%union {
        int cmd;             /* command value */
        char *string;        /* string buffer */
}

%token <cmd> COMMAND ACTION IGNORE EXECUTE ITEM
%token <string> QSTRING
%%
item:   ITEM command action
        ;

command:    /* empty */
          | COMMAND
        ;
```

```
action:    ACTION IGNORE
         | ACTION EXECUTE QSTRING
           ;
    %%
```

While writing the grammar, it became obvious that we still have not given any meaning to our keyword **command**. Indeed, it is often a good idea to try writing the yacc grammar alone, because it can often indicate "holes" in the language design. Fortunately, this is quickly remedied. We will restrict commands to alphanumeric characters—things that look like commands. We need to add recognition of an **ID** token to our lexical analyzer:

```
ws          [ \t]+
qstring     \"[^\"\n]*[\"\n]
id          [a-zA-Z][a-zA-Z0-9]*
nl          \n
%%
{ws}        ;
{qstring}   { yylval.string = yytext;
              return yylval.cmd; }
action      { yylval.cmd = ACTION;
              return yylval.cmd; }
execute     { yylval.cmd = EXECUTE;
              return yylval.cmd; }
choice      { yylval.cmd = CHOICE;
              return yylval.cmd; }
command     { yylval.cmd = COMMAND;
              return yylval.cmd; }
ignore      { yylval.cmd = IGNORE;
              return yylval.cmd; }
{id}        { yylval.string = yytext;
              return ID; }
{nl}        { lineno++; }
.           { return yytext[0]; }
```

Now we can add the **ID** token to our yacc grammar:

```
%{
#include <stdio.h>
%}

%union {
        int cmd;            /* command value */
        char *string;       /* string buffer */
}

%token <cmd> COMMAND ACTION IGNORE EXECUTE ITEM
%token <string> QSTRING ID
%%
item:    ITEM command action
         ;
```

```
command:    /* empty */
          | COMMAND ID
          ;

action:     ACTION IGNORE
          | ACTION EXECUTE QSTRING
          ;
%%
```

If we analyze the above grammar, it further becomes apparent that the grammar does not have any support for more than a single line in a menu. We can define a rule **items** that supports one or more occurrences of **item**:

```
%{
#include <stdio.h>
%}

%union {
        int cmd;                /* command value */
        char *string;           /* string buffer */
}

%token <cmd> COMMAND ACTION IGNORE EXECUTE ITEM
%token <string> QSTRING ID
%%
items: /* empty */
     | items item
     ;

item:    ITEM command action
       ;

command:    /* empty */
          | COMMAND ID
          ;

action:     ACTION IGNORE
          | ACTION EXECUTE QSTRING
          ;
%%
```

Differing from all our previous rules, this one relies upon recursion. Because yacc prefers left-recursive grammars, we wrote "items item" rather than the right-recursive version "item items". For various reasons, the right-recursive version requires additional stack space and, for very large inputs, can cause an overflow condition. Note also that the rule for **items** contains an empty case. Since the second rule is recursive, there must be a terminating condition; if a rule cannot be resolved, yacc will halt with a fatal error, since it is impossible to construct a valid state machine under those circumstances. This left-recursive trick is a common one that you see used many times and in many grammars.

In addition to being able to specify specific items within the menu, it is often desirable to have some type of title at the top of the menu describing the menu. Here is a grammar rule that describes a title:

```
title:          TITLE          QSTRING
       ;
```

We use the keyword **title** to introduce a title and require that the contents of the title line be enclosed in quotation marks. This requires that we add the new token **TITLE** to our lex specification:

```
ws          [ \t]+
qstring     \"[^\"\n]*[\"\n]
id          [a-zA-Z][a-zA-Z0-9]*
nl          \n
%%
{ws}        ;
{qstring}   { yylval.string = yytext;
              return yylval.cmd; }
action      { yylval.cmd = ACTION;
              return yylval.cmd; }
execute     { yylval.cmd = EXECUTE;
              return yylval.cmd; }
choice      { yylval.cmd = CHOICE;
              return yylval.cmd; }
command     { yylval.cmd = COMMAND;
              return yylval.cmd; }
ignore      { yylval.cmd = IGNORE;
              return yylval.cmd; }
title       { yylval.cmd = TITLE;
              return yylval.cmd; }
{id}        { yylval.string = yytext;
              return ID; }
{nl}        { lineno++; }
.           { return yytext[0]; }
```

However, before we add a new rule to our grammar, it seems quite possible that we might want more than a single title line. Our addition to the grammar will consist of two lines:

```
titles:   /* empty */
        | titles title
        ;

title:          TITLE          QSTRING
       ;
```

Once again, we use a recursive definition to allow the addition of multiple title lines.

The addition of title lines does imply that we must add a new, higher-level rule to consist of either items or titles. It seems reasonable to presume that titles will come before items, so we could add a new rule, **start**, to our grammar:

```
%{
#include <stdio.h>
%}

%union {
        int cmd;                    /* command value */
        char *string;               /* string buffer */
}

%token <cmd> COMMAND ACTION IGNORE EXECUTE ITEM TITLE
%token <string> QSTRING ID
%%
start:  titles items
        ;

titles:     /* empty */
        | titles title
        ;

title:          TITLE           QSTRING
        ;

items:  /* empty */
        | items item
        ;

item:     ITEM command action
        ;

command:    /* empty */
        | COMMAND ID
        ;

action:   ACTION IGNORE
        | ACTION EXECUTE QSTRING
        ;
%%
```

After we implemented a menu generator based upon the above, we found it useful to allow several menu screens within a single specification, allowing the menu generator to handle the specifics of how individual menu screens reference other menu screens. This required the addition of the rule **screen**. Each screen could contain a complete menu with both titles and items. After this addition, our grammar became:

```
%{
#include <stdio.h>
%}

%union {
        int cmd;                /* command value */
        char *string;           /* string buffer */
}

%token <cmd> COMMAND ACTION IGNORE EXECUTE ITEM TITLE
%token <string> QSTRING ID
%%
start: screen
        ;

screen: titles items
        ;

titles:    /* empty */
        | titles title
        ;

title:          TITLE           QSTRING
        ;

items:  /* empty */
        | items item
        ;

item:   ITEM command action
        ;

command:   /* empty */
        | COMMAND ID
        ;

action:   ACTION IGNORE
        | ACTION EXECUTE QSTRING
        ;
%%
```

To add the handling of multiple screens we can, once again, use our recursive model to build a new **screens** rule. Thus, our addition to the grammar is:

```
screens:  /* nothing */
        | screens screen
        ;

screen:   screen_name screen_contents screen_terminator
        | screen_name screen_terminator
        ;

screen_name:  SCREEN ID
            | SCREEN
            ;

screen_terminator:  END ID
                  | END
                  ;

screen_contents: titles lines
```

We provide each screen with its own unique name. Thus, when we wish to reference a particular menu screen, say, "foo", we can use a line such as:

```
item "foo" command foo action menu foo
```

When we decide to name screens, however, we must also indicate when a screen ends, which explains the reasoning behind the **screen_terminator** rule. Thus, a sample screen specification might be:

```
screen foo
title "Foo"
item "foo" command foo action ignore
item "bar" command bar action execute "/bin/sh"
end foo
screen bar
title "Bar"
item "bar" command bar action menu foo
item "foo" command foo action quit
end bar
```

Note that our rule *does* provide for the case when no name is given; hence, the two cases for **screen_name** and **screen_terminator**. When we actually write actions for the specific rules, it will be desirable to check that the names are consistent—to prevent partial editing of a menu description buffer, for instance.

After some additional thought, we decided to add a single additional feature to our menu generation language. For each item, we wish to indicate if it is *visible* or *invisible*. Since we think of this as an attribute of the individual item, we preface the choice of visible/invisible with the new keyword **attribute**. Here is the portion of our new grammar that describes an attribute:

```
attribute: /* empty */
        | ATTRIBUTE VISIBLE
        | ATTRIBUTE INVISIBLE
        ;
```

We allow the attribute field to be empty and thus accept some default, probably *visible*. With these changes, we now have a workable version of the grammar:

```
screens:  /* nothing */
        | screens screen
        ;

screen:   screen_name screen_contents screen_terminator
        | screen_name screen_terminator
        | screen_name error screen_terminator
        ;

screen_name:  SCREEN ID
            | SCREEN
            ;

screen_terminator:  END ID
                  | END
                  ;

screen_contents: titles lines
               ;

titles: /* empty */
      | titles title
      ;

title: TITLE QSTRING
     ;

lines:    /* empty */
      | lines line
      ;

line: ITEM QSTRING command ACTION action attribute
    ;


command:  /* empty */
        | COMMAND ID
        ;
```

```
action:     EXECUTE QSTRING
          | MENU ID
          | QUIT
          | IGNORE
          ;

attribute:  /* empty */
          | ATTRIBUTE VISIBLE
          | ATTRIBUTE INVISIBLE
          ;
```

We have replaced the **start** rule of previous examples with our **screens** rule; the actual name of the starting routine is immaterial to yacc. If there is no rule specified by the **%start** directive in the declarations section, it simply uses the first rule.

Building the MGL

Now that we have a basic grammar, the work of actually building the compiler begins. First, we must finish modifying our lexical analyzer to cope with the new keywords we introduced in our last round of grammar changes. Our modified lex specification is shown in Example 4-1.

Example 4-1. MGL lex specification

```
w          [ \t]+
real       [0-9]+.[0-9]+
integer    [0-9]+
comment    ^#*$
qstring    \"[^\"\n]*[\"\n]
id         [a-zA-Z][a-zA-Z0-9]*
nl         \n

%%

{ws}       ;
{real}     { sscanf(yytext,"%lf",&yylval.real);
             return REAL; }
{integer}  { sscanf(yytext,"%d", &yylval.integer);
             return INTEGER; }
{comment}  { yylval.string = yytext;
             return COMMENT; }
{qstring}  { yylval.string = yytext;
             if(yylval.string[strlen(yylval.string)-1] != '"')
               warning("Unterminated character string",(char *)0);
             return QSTRING; }
screen     { yylval.cmd = SCREEN;
             return yylval.cmd; }
title      { yylval.cmd = TITLE;
```

Example 4-1. MGL lex specification (continued)

```
                return yylval.cmd; }
item          { yylval.cmd = ITEM;
                return yylval.cmd; }
command       { yylval.cmd = COMMAND;
                return yylval.cmd; }
action        { yylval.cmd = ACTION;
                return yylval.cmd; }
execute       { yylval.cmd = EXECUTE;
                return yylval.cmd; }
menu          { yylval.cmd = MENU;
                return yylval.cmd; }
quit          { yylval.cmd = QUIT;
                return yylval.cmd; }
ignore        { yylval.cmd = IGNORE;
                return yylval.cmd; }
attribute     { yylval.cmd = ATTRIBUTE;
                return yylval.cmd; }
visible       { yylval.cmd = VISIBLE;
                return yylval.cmd; }
invisible     { yylval.cmd = INVISIBLE;
                return yylval.cmd; }
end           { yylval.cmd = END;
                return yylval.cmd; }
{id}          { yylval.string = yytext;
                return ID;}
{nl}          { lineno++; }
.             { return yytext[0]; }
%%
```

An alternative implementation is demonstrated in Example 4-2.

Example 4-2. Alternative lex specification

```
ws         [ \t]+
real       [0-9]+.[0-9]+
integer    [0-9]+
comment    ^#*$
qstring    \"[^\"\n]*\"
id         [a-zA-Z][a-zA-Z0-9]*
nl         \n

%%

{ws}       ;
{real}     { sscanf(yytext,"%lf",&yylval.real);
             return REAL; }
{integer}  { sscanf(yytext,"%d", &yylval.integer);
             return INTEGER; }
{comment}  { yylval.string = yytext;
             return COMMENT; }
{qstring}  { yylval.string = yytext;
```

Example 4-2. Alternative lex specification (continued)

```
                return QSTRING; }
{id}        { if(yylval.cmd = keyword(yytext)) return yylval.cmd;
                yylval.string = yytext;
                return ID;
}
{nl}        { lineno++; }
.           { return yytext[0]; }
%%
/*
 * keyword: Take a text string and determine if it is, in fact,
 * a valid keyword.  If it is, return the value of the keyword;
 * if not, return zero.  N.B.:  The token values must be nonzero.
 */

static struct keyword {
char *name;      /* text string */
int value;       /* token */
int length;      /* length of name */
} keywords[] =
{
"screen",     SCREEN,  6,
"title",      TITLE,  5,
"item",       ITEM, 4,
"command",    COMMAND,  7,
"action",     ACTION,  6,
"execute",    EXECUTE,  7,
"menu",       MENU,  4,
"quit",       QUIT,  4,
"ignore",     IGNORE,  6,
"attribute",  ATTRIBUTE,  9,
"visible",    VISIBLE,  7,
"invisible",  INVISIBLE,  9,
"end",        END,  3,
(char *)0,  0,  0,
};

int keyword(string)
   char *string;
   {
   struct keyword *ptr = keywords;
   int len = strlen(string);

#ifdef KEY_CHECK
   fprintf(stderr,"%s: checking keywords\n",progname);
   while(ptr->length != 0)
      {
        if(strlen(ptr->name) != ptr->length)
   {
     fprintf(stderr,"keyword %s, length is %d should be %d\n",
     ptr->name, strlen(ptr->name), ptr->length);
   }
```

Example 4-2. Alternative lex specification (continued)

```
        ptr++;
    }
    fprintf(stderr,"%s: done checking keywords,ok\n",progname);
    ptr = keywords;
#endif /* KEY_CHECK */

    while(ptr->length != 0)
        if(len == ptr->length && (strcmp(ptr->name,string) == 0))
            {
#ifdef DEBUG
    fprintf(stderr,"%s: returning keyword # %d\n",progname,
    ptr->value);
#endif
    return ptr->value;
}
        else
            {
#ifdef DEBUG
        fprintf(stderr,"%s: %s (%d) != %s (%d)\n",
                    progname,ptr->name, ptr->length,
                    string,len);
#endif
        ptr++;
        }

    return 0; /* no match */
}
```

This alternate implementation uses a static table from which keywords are searched; for some versions of lex, the alternate version proves to be faster. We choose to include it here simply because it demonstrates a useful technique that could be used if we wished to make the language *extensible*, such as C is. In that case, we would need only a single lookup mechanism for *all keywords*.

Logically, we can divide the work in processing a compilation file into several parts:

Initialization   This stage includes initializing all internal data tables as well as emitting any preambles needed for the code that we will be generating.

Start-of-screen processing   This stage includes setting up a new state-table entry, adding the name of the screen to the list, and emitting our initial screen code.

Screen processing   Now as we encounter individual items, we will need to perform additional processing; e.g., when we see title lines, we need to deal with them, and when we see new menu items, we will insert them into our list.

End-of-screen processing   Once the **end** statement has been seen, we can process the data structures we have built and emit code for that particular screen.

Termination   At this stage, we need to "clean up" the internal state, emit any postamble, and assure that this termination is OK; if there is a problem, it must be reported to the user.

Initialization

Normally, there is a certain amount of work that must typically be performed when *any* compiler begins operation. For instance, internal data structures must be initialized; recall that Example 4-2 used a keyword lookup scheme rather than the hardcoded keyword recognition scheme used earlier in Example 4-1. For this case, we could simply use a static array; in general, however, this will not work. For this scheme, we must call the initialization routine initially so that the keyword data table can, in fact, be initialized. (Alternatively, we can simply check a static variable to determine if initialization has occurred. This is unacceptable if the routine will be called *too* frequently, because of the expense of the extra comparison.)

Our **main** routine will start out simply:

```
main()
  {
    yyparse();
  }
```

However, we must also be able to invoke our compiler by providing it directly with a file name. Because lex reads from the standard input and writes occur (by default) to the standard output, we need merely reattach the input/output pipes to obtain the appropriate action. This is accomplished by using the *freopen* call provided by UNIX. The following code fragment demonstrates how to reattach *stdin*, the standard input:

```
  {
  FILE *in;
  char *infile = "foo";
    in = freopen(infile,"r",stdin); /* open for read */
    if(in == NULL)                   /* open failed */
      {
            fprintf(stderr,"cannot open %s\n", infile);
            exit(EX_NOINPUT);
      }
  }
```

In constructing our redirection code, we will assume the following:

- If the user invokes the program with zero arguments, we will write out to a default file, say, *screen.out*, and use the standard input, *stdin*, as the default input source.

- If the user invokes the program with one argument, we will still write out to our default file *screen.out* and use the named file as the input by reattaching it to *stdin*.

- If the user invokes the program with two arguments, we will write out to the file named as the *first* argument, using the *second* argument as the name of the input file; both will be reattached to their appropriate *stdin/stdout* counterparts.

After we return from the **yyparse** call, we need to perform any necessary postprocessing and then check to assure we are terminating outside of an error condition. We then perform any necessary cleanup and exit.

Our resulting **main** routine looks like this:

```
char *progname = "menugen";
int lineno = 1;

#include "menu_lex.c"
#include <sysexits.h>

#define DEFAULT_OUTFILE "screen.out"

char *usage = "%s: usage <outfile> <infile>\n";

main(argc,argv)
    int argc;
    char **argv;
  {
    char *outfile;
    char *infile;

    progname = argv[0];

    if(argc > 3)
      {
        fprintf(stderr,usage, progname);
        exit(EX_USAGE);
      }
    if(argc > 1)
      {
        outfile = argv[1];
        if(argc > 2)
          {
            infile = argv[2];
            /* open for read */
```

```
            in = freopen(infile,"r",stdin);
            if(in == NULL) /* open failed */
                {
                    fprintf(stderr,"%s: cannot open %s\n",
                            progname, infile);
                    exit(EX_NOINPUT);
                }
            }
        else in = stdin;
        }
    else
        {
            outfile = DEFAULT_OUTFILE;
            in = stdin;
        }

    out = freopen(outfile,"w",stdout);
    if(out == NULL) /* open failed */
        {
            fprintf(stderr,"%s: cannot open %s\n",
                    progname, outfile);
            exit(EX_CANTCREAT);
        }

    /* normal interaction on stdin and
       stdout from now on... */

    yyparse();

    end_file(); /* write out any final information */

    /* tidy up */
    fclose(out);
    fclose(in);

    /* now check EOF condition */
    if(!screen_done) /* in the middle of a screen */
        {
            warning("Premature EOF",(char *)0);
            unlink(outfile); /* remove bad file */
            exit(EX_DATAERR);
        }
    exit(0); /* no error */
}
```

Screen Processing

Once we have initialized the compiler to attach to the appropriate files, we turn our attention to the *real* work of the menu generator—that of processing the menu descriptions themselves. Our first rule, **screens**, requires no actions. Our **screen** rule decomposes into the parts **screen_name**, **screen_contents**, and **screen_terminator**. It is **screen_name** that interests us first:

```
screen_name:   SCREEN ID
             | SCREEN
             ;
```

We need to insert the specified name into our list of names (to prevent collision); in case no name is specified, we will use the name "default". Our rule then becomes:

```
screen_name:   SCREEN ID   { start_screen($2); }
             | SCREEN      { start_screen("default"); }
             ;
```

The **start_screen** routine should enter the name into our list of screens and begin to generate the code. For instance, if our input file said "screen foo", the **start_screen** routine would produce the following code:

```
/* screen foo */
menu_foo()
{
        extern struct item menu_foo_items[];

        if(!init) menu_init();

        clear();
        refresh();
```

Now when processing our menu specification, the next object we see is a title line:

```
title: TITLE QSTRING
       ;
```

We call our routine **add_title**, which computes the positioning for the title line:

```
title: TITLE QSTRING { add_title($2); }
       ;
```

Our sample output for title lines looks like this:

```
move(0,37);
addstr("Foo");
refresh();
```

We add a title line by positioning the cursor and printing out the requested quoted string (note that we do some rudimentary centering here as well). This code can be repeated for each title line we encounter; the only change we must make is to the line number that we are currently using to generate the move instruction.

To demonstrate this, we modify our original test menu description to include an extra title line:

```
screen foo
title "Foo"
title "Copyright 1990"
item "foo" command foo action ignore attribute visible
item "bar" command bar action execute "/bin/sh" attribute visible
end foo
screen bar
title "Bar"
item "bar" command bar action menu foo attribute visible
item "foo" command foo action quit attribute invisible
end bar
```

Our sample output for title lines then appears as:

```
addstr("Foo");
refresh();
move(1,32);
addstr("Copyright 1990");
refresh();
```

Once we begin to see a list of item lines, we must take the individual entries and build an internal *table* of the associated actions. This continues until the **end foo** statement is seen, at which time we perform post-processing and finish building this particular screen. To build a table of these menu items, we add the following action to the **item** rule:

```
line:   ITEM qstring {
            if(strlen($2) > sizeof(item_str))
                warning("item string overflow", (char *)0);
            bzero(item_str, sizeof item_str);
            strncpy(item_str,$2, sizeof item_str);
        }
    command ACTION action attribute
        { add_line($6, $7); $$ = $1; }
        ;
```

This action takes the quoted string, copies it into the static buffer **item_str**, and then continues with the parsing of the rule. After the full rule has been reduced, *then* the routine **add_line** is called to add the specified line to the menu item table. The intermediate action is necessary in this case because the lexical analyzer is not returning the token in allocated space—rather it is using the input buffer directly. What this means is that were we to reference rule "$2", where we have the **add_line**, the *quoted string* would no longer exist, because the input buffer would now contain the current position within the input buffer! Thus, by copying it out upon detection, we avoid losing this information.

The rules for **command, action,** and **attribute** also perform some function as well:

```
command:   /* empty */
            { bzero(cmd_str, sizeof cmd_str);
              $$ = EMPTY;}
        | COMMAND id
            { if (strlen($2) > sizeof cmd_str)
                  warning("command string overflow",
                          (char *)0);
              bzero(cmd_str,sizeof cmd_str);
              strncpy(cmd_str, $2, sizeof cmd_str);
              $$ = $1; }
```

For **command**, we specify an empty string (i.e., we have no command entered) and its action empties the buffer **cmd_str** or a command and its action copies the contents of the input buffer into the buffer **cmd_str**. We return the value **EMPTY** in the former case and **COMMAND** in the latter.

The **action** rule and the associated actions are a bit more complex, partially because of the larger number of variations possible:

```
action: EXECUTE qstring
          { if (strlen($2) > sizeof act_str)
                warning("action string overflow", (char *)0);
            bzero(act_str,sizeof act_str);
            strncpy(act_str, $2, sizeof act_str); $$ = $1; }
      | MENU id
          { if (strlen($2) > (sizeof(act_str) - 5))
            warning("action string overflow", (char *)0);
            bzero(act_str,sizeof act_str);
            strcpy(act_str,"menu_");
            strncat(act_str, $2, sizeof(act_str)-5);
            $$ = $1; }
      | QUIT
          { $$ = $1; }
      | IGNORE
          { $$ = $1; }
      ;
```

Finally, the **attribute** rule proves to be straightforward, as the only semantic value is represented by the particular token itself:

```
attribute:  /* empty */               { $$ = VISIBLE; }
          | ATTRIBUTE VISIBLE         { $$ = $2; }
          | ATTRIBUTE INVISIBLE       { $$ = $2; }
          ;
```

Now recall that the return values of the **action** rule and the **attribute** rule were passed to the **add_line** routine; this call takes the contents of the various static buffers, plus the two return values, and creates an entry in the internal state table.

Upon seeing the **end foo** statement, we must begin the final processing of the screen. From our sample output, we finish the **menu_foo** routine:

```
        menu_runtime(menu_foo_items);
}
```

The actual menu items are then written into the **menu_foo_items** array:

```
/* end foo */
struct item menu_foo_items[]={
{"bar","bar",267,"/bin/sh",0,273},
{"foo","foo",271,"",0,273},
{(char *)0, (char *)0, 0, (char *)0, 0, 0},
};
```

The actual run-time routine **menu_runtime** will be responsible for handling the specifics of displaying the individual items; this will be included in the generated file as part of the post-processing run (although it could also have been included in the preamble as well).

Termination

The final stage of dealing with a single screen is to see the termination of that screen. Recall our **screen** rule:

```
screen:   screen_name screen_contents screen_terminator
        | screen_name screen_terminator
        | screen_name error screen_terminator
        ;
```

The grammar then expects to see the **screen_terminator** rule:

```
screen_terminator:  END ID
                  | END
                  ;
```

We need to add a call to our post-processing routine; this is the *end-of-screen* post-processing, not the end-of-file post-processing (which we will discuss later in this section). Here is the resulting rule with actions that we had:

```
screen_terminator:  END ID     { end_screen($2); }
                  | END        { end_screen("default"); }
                  ;
```

It calls the routine **end_screen** with the name of the screen (or "default", if no name is provided). This routine would then do screen-name checking. For example, the code we used to implement this looks like:

```
   /*
    * end_screen:
    * Finish screen, print out postamble.
    */

end_screen(name)
   char *name;
  {

     printf("\tmenu_runtime(menu_%s_items);\n", name);

     if(strcmp(current_screen,name) != 0)
       {
          warning("name mismatch at end of screen", (char *)0);
       }
     printf("}\n");
     printf("/* end %s */\n",current_screen);

     process_items();

     /* write initialization code out to file */
     if(!done_end_init)
       {
          done_end_init = 1;
          dump_data(menu_init);
       }

     bzero(current_screen, sizeof current_screen);

     screen_done = 1;

     return 0;
  }
```

One interesting feature of this routine is its *nonfatal* handling of a screen name mismatch. Since name matching at the *end* of a screen does *not* cause problems within the state of the compiler, it can be reported to the user *without* termination.

This routine processes the state generated by our **add_item** call while processing individual item entries with the call to **process_items**. Then this routine writes out some initialization routines with the call to **dump_data**; these initialization routines are really just a static array of strings that are determined at compile time. This is why the **dump_data** call is used several times to dump different code fragments to the output file. An alternative approach is to simply copy these code fragments from some skeleton file, much as lex and yacc do.

Our final responsibility is to handle the post-processing section after all input has been read and parsed. This is done by the **main** routine after **yyparse** has completed successfully with the call to **end_file**. Our sample implementation looked like this:

```
end_file()
{
static ef_called = 0;

if(ef_called)
{
warning("Internal error: end_file called twice\n");
exit(EX_SOFTWARE);
}
ef_called = 1;

dump_data(menu_runtime);
}
```

This routine contains a basic internal consistency check (that it is not called twice) plus a single call to **dump_data** with the runtime routines, which, as with the initialization code, are stored in a compile-time array. All our routines that handle the boiler-plate code are sufficiently "modular" in design that these could be rewritten to use skeleton files.

Once this routine has been called, the **main** routine terminates by closing the various files, checking to determine if EOF was detected at a valid point (e.g., at a screen boundary) and, if not, generating an appropriate error message.

Sample MGL Code

Now that we have built a sample compiler, we would like to demonstrate the basic workings of it. Our implementation of the MGL consisted of three parts: the yacc grammar, the lex specification, and our supporting code routines (the true internals of the compiler). The final version of our yacc grammar with additional changes is shown in Appendix E, *MGL Compiler Code*. The final version of our lex specification is also shown in Appendix E.

We do not consider the sample code to be robust enough for serious use; our attention was given to developing a first-stage implementation. The resulting compiler will, however, generate a fully functional menu compiler. Here is our sample input file:

```
screen foo
title "Foo"
item "foo" command foo action ignore attribute visible
item "bar" command bar action execute "/bin/sh" attribute visible
end foo
screen bar
title "Bar"
item "bar" command bar action menu foo attribute visible
item "foo" command foo action quit attribute invisible
end bar
```

When that description file was processed by our compiler, we got the following output file:

```
/*
 * Generated by MGL: Wed Nov 29 17:25:56 1989
 */

/* initialization information */
static int init;

#include <curses.h>
#include <sys/signal.h>
#include <ctype.h>
#include <sysexits.h>
#include "menu_yacc.h"

/* structure used to store menu items */
struct item {
char *desc;
char *cmd;
int  action;
char   *act_str;      /* execute string */
int (*act_menu)();    /* call appropriate function */
```

```
int   attribute;
};

/* screen foo */
menu_foo()
{
  extern struct item menu_foo_items[];

  if(!init) menu_init();

  clear();
  refresh();
  move(0,37);
  addstr("Foo");
  refresh();
  menu_runtime(menu_foo_items);
}
/* end foo */
struct item menu_foo_items[]={
  {"bar","bar",267,"/bin/sh",0,273},
  {"foo","foo",271,"",0,273},
  {(char *)0, (char *)0, 0, (char *)0, 0, 0},
  };

menu_init()
  {
    int menu_cleanup();

    signal(SIGINT, menu_cleanup);
    initscr();
    crmode();
  }


menu_cleanup()
  {
    mvcur(0, COLS - 1, LINES - 1, 0);
    endwin();
  }

  /* screen bar */
  menu_bar()
  {
    extern struct item menu_bar_items[];

    if(!init) menu_init();

    clear();
    refresh();
    move(0,37);
    addstr("Bar");
    refresh();
    menu_runtime(menu_bar_items);
```

```
   }
   /* end bar */
struct item menu_bar_items[]={
   {"foo","foo",270,"",0,274},
   {"bar","bar",269,"",menu_foo,273},
   {(char *)0, (char *)0, 0, (char *)0, 0, 0},
   };

/* runtime */

menu_runtime(items)
   struct item *items;
   {
     unsigned count,visible,invisible,index;
     struct item *ptr;
     char buf[BUFSIZ];
     unsigned choice = 0;

     for(ptr = items; ptr->desc != 0; ptr++)
if(ptr->attribute == VISIBLE) visible++;
else invisible++;

     count = visible+invisible;
     for(ptr = items,index = 1; ptr->desc != 0;
         ptr++,index++) {
addch('\n'); /* skip a line */
         printw("\t%d) %s",index,ptr->desc);
       }

     addstr("\n\n\t"); /* tab out so it looks "nice" */
     refresh();

     while(1)
       {
while(1)
  {
             getstr(buf);

             /*
              * Check for a valid response.  It must be
              * either:
              * (a) a numeric choice within the visible
              *     range or
              * (b) a command matching one in the list.
              */

             sscanf(buf,"%d\n",&choice);
             if(choice > 0 && choice <= visible)
         break;
           }

                 if(choice != 0) /* numeric choice */
                   {
```

```
            int i;

            for(i = 1, ptr = items; ptr->desc != 0 &&
                       i < choice; ptr++)
        if(ptr->attribute == VISIBLE) i++;
            if(ptr->attribute != 0) /* valid choice */
                {
        switch(ptr->action)
            {
        case QUIT:
            return 0;
        case IGNORE:
            refresh();
            break;
        case EXECUTE:
            refresh();
            execl(ptr->act_str,0);
            break;
        case MENU:
            refresh();
            (*ptr->act_menu)();
            break;
        default:
            printw("default case, no action\n");
            refresh();
            break;
        }
                }
                    }
        refresh();
                }
            }

#define ALLOC(x,s,t) \
do { x = (t)calloc(1,(s)); if (x == 0)\
        { fprintf(stderr,"memory allocation failed",\
  (char *)0); exit(EX_OSERR); } } while(0)\

casecmp(string1,string2)
    char *string1,*string2;
  {
    char *p,*q,*r;
    int result;

    ALLOC(p,strlen(string1)+1,char *);
    ALLOC(q,strlen(string2)+1,char *);

    strcpy(string1,p);
    strcpy(string2,q);

    for(r = p; *r != 0; r++)
*r = (isupper(*r) ? tolower(*r) : *r);
```

```
    for(r = q; *r != 0; r++)
*r = (isupper(*r) ? tolower(*r) : *r);

    result = strcmp(p,q);
    free(p);
    free(q);
    return result;
}
```

In turn, we compiled this code, generated by our compiler and written to *Foo.c*, with the following command:

```
$ cat Foo.c
main()
{
menu_bar();
}
^D
$ cc -o Foo Foo.c -lcurses -ltermcap
$
```

Note that it was necessary to add a **main** routine to the default code; in a revision of the MGL, it might be desirable to include a command line option and/or a specification option to provide a *name* of a routine to call from within the main loop; this is only one of the possible enhancements. Because we wrote our grammar in yacc, this type of modification should prove to be fairly straightforward. For example, we might modify the **screens** rule to read:

```
screens:   /* nothing */
         | preamble screens screen
         | screens screen
         ;

preamble: START ID
        | START DEFAULT
        ;
```

where we add appropriate keywords for **START** and **DEFAULT**.

Running our MGL-generated screen code, we are with the following menu screen:

```
                Bar
1) foo
2) bar
```

As we chose the options on the menu, the appropriate actions were performed. At this stage, we declare our initial implementation a success.

5

The SGL

Designing the SGL
Describing the SGL
Using Lex to Implement SGL
Using Yacc to Implement SGL
Intermediate Languages

This chapter expands upon our development of the MGL by presenting a more complex example, the *screen generation language (SGL)*. First, we will begin by discussing the *reasons* for certain specific language features; later we will turn our attention to actually developing lex and yacc specifications.

Designing the SGL

The MGL functions as the basis from which to design the SGL. We begin by defining a *screen* as a collection of *fields*. Fields may be grouped together and referred to as *regions*. Screens, however, are more complex than menus in that they frequently come in groups. This is usually because a *logical screen* cannot fit on a *physical screen*. Of course, physical screens are not guaranteed to all be the same size. In fact, a physical screen can change size *while running*. This is becoming much more common in a window-based workstation environment. Thus, a good screen generator should be able to handle a wide range of contingencies with a high degree of flexibility. This does mean, however, that the user will give up some of the control over the screen's particular layout (as it must be computed at *run time*).

So each screen is of *arbitrary size*—the screen generator will handle the complexities of breaking an individual screen into multiple screens. It would appear, then, that the next thing to do (after discussing the general characteristics) is to develop a model of how the SGL specification file should look. First, the SGL file should begin with a declaration of the screen name, similar to that used in the MGL. However, since there are regions as well as screens, they too should be declared (and named). Here is a first pass at the layout of the SGL file:

```
screen foo title bar end bar

region one end one

region two end two

end foo
```

An alternative might be:

```
begin screen foo begin title bar end title bar

begin region one end region one

begin region two end region two

end screen foo
```

Although the second version is perhaps more consistent looking, it appears more cumbersome to use. Since it does not seem to give any great benefit (aside from an aesthetic view), the first form will be used.

The goal at this stage is to develop a grammar in which it is relatively "certain" at each stage what is being analyzed. Hence, the point for clearly delineating what is currently being processed. This can be done by using begin/end pairs to denote a block and subidentifiers to denote the type of block. This helps in building the parser and in error detection.

The title is a limited form of region; it displays information. With that view in mind, a title's capabilities will be examined after those of the region have been described. A region is made up of *fields*. Each field must have an associated *variable* in the surrounding program (defined by the user). Additionally, each field must have an associated *type*. Since it is often necessary to provide limitations upon the *range* of a variable, it must have a *range* option and a *size*.

Most of the options for a field, then, are fairly simple. The one difficult portion is validation (for the type and range). There are two ways to handle this: either by predefining the types allowed or by allowing a declaration of types. The first possibility is "easier" from the implementation standpoint, but the second is better from the perspective of the user. A reasonable compromise is to allow definition of an arbitrary type but to have *predefined* types. A type must provide the name of an integer function that will accept three character-pointer arguments: a buffer containing the user input, a lower bound, and an upper bound. The lower and upper bounds can be null pointers (indicating there is no bound in the specified direction). The fourth argument will be a pointer to the variable in which the converted argument is to be placed. The return values have the meanings set out in Table 5-1. Of course, the error return values should be set out as symbolic constants in an appropriate header file.

Table 5-1: SGL Type Handling Function Return Values

Return Value	Meaning
-3	Underflow (out of bounds)
-2	Overflow (out of bounds)
-1	Improper invocation (bad argument)
0	Successful conversion

A reasonable collection of data types would be:

- Character strings
- Integers
- Dates
- Monetary amounts
- Boolean fields

Since it is possible to extend this list, it seems wise to keep it small. Each *type*, then, must be declared (except the default types, which are implicitly declared by the SGL system). A sample declaration of the default types might be:

```
type string string_checker
type integer integer_checker
type date date_checker
type money money_checker
type boolean boolean_checker
```

where the second field is the *type name* and the last field is the name of the routine to call for verification of the data entry.

It now appears that the basic layout for a field has been defined. Here is an informal syntax for the field entry of an SGL screen:

field <variable_name> type <type_name>
[lower bound <lbound>] [upper bound <ubound>]
[size <size_value>]

Given this definition, a sample field is:

```
field foo type string
```

Now putting all the previous discussion together, a sample SGL file for a simple telephone/address database's front-end is shown in Example 5-1.

Example 5-1. SGL sample telephone database front-end

```
begin telephone
      type phoneno phoneno_checker
      type state state_checker
      type zip zip_checker

      title
          "Telephone Inquiry Program"
"Version 1.0"
      end

      region main
          field phone.lastname type string size 15
      field phone.fullname type string size 45
      field phone.addr.line1 type string size 30
      field phone.addr.line2 type string size 30
      field phone.addr.city type string size 20
      field phone.addr.state type state size 2
      field phone.addr.zip type zip size 9
      field phone.phonenum type phoneno size 11
          end main

      end telephone
```

Describing the SGL

Now that an informal notion of the SGL has been defined, it must be formalized into a set of production rules. These production rules can then be used in the next section to build the yacc grammar.

Just as the informal description was done from the "outside" in, so is the formal description. First, then, a screen would be:

> *screen* ← **begin id** *screen_contents* **end id**

where **id** is any valid identifier (that is not a keyword). The declaration for the internals is:

> *screen_contents* ← *type_list title regions*

Now the *type_list* will use left recursion in its definition:

> *type_list* ← *type_list type*
> *type* ← **type id id**

Although this could have been defined right-recursively, the left recursion is used to keep with yacc's preference for left-recursive grammars. Continuing with this development, a title is defined as:

> *title* ← **begin title** *title_lines* **end title**
> *title_lines* ← *title_lines title_line*
> *title_line* **title qstring**

where **qstring** is any quoted string. Similarly for a region:

> *regions* ← *regions region*
> *region* ← **begin region id** *fields* **end region id**

Finally, the definition of the fundamental block—the field:

> *fields* ← *fields field*
> *field* ← **field id type id** *bounds size*
> *bounds* ← *lower_bound upper_bound*
> *lower_bound* ← ε | **lower bound qstring**
> *upper_bound* ← ε | **upper bound qstring**
> *size* ← ε | **size integer**

(where ε indicates an empty definition).

The lower and upper bounds take *quoted strings* rather than an **ID**, because it is quite possible they may be numbers. If that is the case, the lexical analyzer would convert them to numeric form—not what is desired. This protects them from interpretation by the lexical analyzer (instead the data checking routine must convert them appropriately).

In the remainder of this chapter, we will concentrate upon developing lex and yacc specifications for the SGL; because of the greater complexity of this project, we will not discuss the supporting C that implements implementation of actions, etc.

Using Lex to Implement SGL

First, we will need a good lexical analyzer to tokenize the input stream. The SGL is similar to the MGL, so the lexical analyzer will be similar as well. Indeed, for many purposes, the lexical analyzer we have demonstrated here can be used for a great number of implementations. We start with a set of definitions:

```
ws        [ \t]+
real      [0-9]+.[0-9]+
integer   [0-9]+
comment   ^#*$
qstring   \"[^\"\n]*\"
id        [_a-zA-Z][\._a-zA-Z0-9]*
nl        \n
```

ws is whitespace, which is ignored. **real** describes real numbers in decimal form; they are not used in the SGL. **integers** are arbitrary length integer numbers. It is possible that they may not *fit* in the integer representation of the machine. One technique to deal with this situation is to ignore and silently truncate; another is to generate a warning message. A **comment** allows embedding of comments inside the source text. Although we do not use preprocessor commands in the SGL, it might be desirable to do so. For instance, if we wished to add C-style includes, we might define such as being:

```
preproc   ^#include*$
```

Of course, this would introduce an ambiguity, because **preproc** is a subset of **comment**. Such ambiguity, however, can be handled by lex with little difficulty.

qstring is any string inside quotes, while **id** is any valid identifier. Note that unlike the MGL, the SGL allows the underscore (_) anywhere in the identifier and the period inside the identifier. This fits the definition of C identifiers (and since we presume many variable names will be C identifiers, we will rely upon this support). However, this also broadens the range of SGL identifiers; it may be more desirable to add a separate definition of a C identifier, resulting in:

```
id    [a-zA-Z][a-zA-Z0-9]*
cid   [_a-zA-Z][\._a-zA-Z0-9]*
```

Then the yacc grammar could recognize both an **ID** and a **CID** as appropriate. However, we will use only the single type of identifier for simplicity.

Finally, we define **nl** to be the newline character. These definitions, although simple, form the basis for the rules of our basic lexical analyzer.

Here is the lexical analyzer used for the MGL. The one for SGL will be almost identical:

```
{ws}            ;
{real}          { sscanf(yytext,"%lf",&yylval.real);
                  return REAL; }
{integer}       { sscanf(yytext,"%d", &yylval.integer);
                  return INTEGER; }
{comment}       { yylval.string = yytext;
                  return COMMENT; }
{qstring}       { yylval.string = yytext;
                  return QSTRING; }
{id}            { if(yylval.cmd = keyword(yytext))
                      return yylval.cmd;
                  yylval.string = yytext;
                  return ID;
                }
{nl}            { lineno++; }
.               { return yytext[0]; }
```

Recall that in the previous chapter, we found it necessary to save strings in global variables as they were recognized. The rules for **comment**, **qstring**, and **id** should make clear why. The lex variable **yytext** is the text of the current token being parsed. By "pointing" at that buffer, the parser will see the value of the current token (this is done by the line "yylval.string = yytext;"), but the next time lex uses this buffer (to continue analyzing the input stream, for example), the contents will be destroyed. Another alternative was suggested in the previous chapter—use allocated memory. We will use this scheme for the SGL. Here are the declarations and rules of a lex specification that is doing exactly that:

```
%{
char *calloc();

#define ALLOC(x,s,t)   do { x = (t)calloc(1,(s)); \
        if (x == (t)0) { \
            warning("memory allocation failed",\
                    (char *)0);\
            exit(1); } } while(0)
#ifdef BSD
#define BCOPY(from,to,size)  bcopy(from,to,size)
#else
#define BCOPY(from,to,size)  memcpy(to,from,size);
#endif
#define NEWSTR(from,to) do { int len = strlen(from);\
                             ALLOC(to, len+1, char *);\
                             BCOPY(from,to,len+1);\
                           } while(0)
%}
ws      [ \t]+
real    [0-9]+.[0-9]+
integer [0-9]+
```

```
comment   ^#*$
qstring   \"[^\"\n]*\"
id        [_a-zA-Z][\._a-zA-Z0-9]*
nl        \n

%%

{ws}              ;
{real}            { sscanf(yytext,"%lf",&yylval.real);
                    return REAL; }
{integer}         { sscanf(yytext,"%d", &yylval.integer);
                    return INTEGER; }
{comment}         { NEWSTR(yytext,yylval.string);
                    return COMMENT; }
{qstring}         { NEWSTR(yytext,yylval.string);
                    return QSTRING; }
{id}              {
                    if(yylval.cmd = keyword(yytext))
                       return yylval.cmd;
                    NEWSTR(yytext,yylval.string);
                    return ID;
                  }
{nl}              { lineno++; }
.                 { return yytext[0]; }
```

Most of the work is done in the two macros **ALLOC** and **NEWSTR**. We chose to do the actual work with macros so that the rules section would not become cluttered with unnecessary C code. After all, the rudiments of allocating dynamic memory are easily handled by these simple macros. This leaves us with a rules section that clearly shows *what* it does without forcing us to remember exactly *how*. This is a very useful technique in general and specifically with lex (and yacc) specifications. The simpler the rules are to understand, the easier future work on the overall program will be.

The greatest advantage to this dynamic allocation is in the yacc grammar's complexity (which we will discuss in the next section). Because it limits the use of global variables, it also makes program flow more understandable (and debugging easier). In addition, certain classes of programs experience a significant overhead for global data; for instance, this is true of any multi-threaded program.

The burden, however, will be upon the routines accepting those arguments to free the memory; otherwise, the compiler will fail due to memory exhaustion. The worst aspect of this will be that such memory problems will not show up on a small or even a medium test. Indeed, the problem will most likely manifest itself at some future point upon a large file. Although this might not happen with the SGL, it could with a C compiler.

The code section for the lexical analyzer would be identical to that previously used for the MGL, with the substitution of the appropriate keywords. Here is the SGL code section:

```
/*
 * keyword:  Take a text string and determine if it
 * is, in fact, a valid keyword.  If it is, return
 * the value of the keyword; if not, return zero.
 * N.B.:  The token values must be nonzero.
 */

static struct keyword {
     char     *name;             /* text string */
     int       value;            /* token */
     int       length;           /* length of name */
} keywords[]  =
{
"screen",      SCREEN,      6,
"type",        TYPE,        4,
"title",       TITLE,       5,
"region",      REGION,      6,
"field",       FIELD        5,
"lower",       LOWER        5,
"upper",       UPPER        5,
"bound",       BOUND        5,
"size",        SIZE         4,
"end",         END,         3,
(char *)0,     0,           0,
};

int keyword(string)
   char *string;
  {
    struct keyword *ptr = keywords;
    int len = strlen(string);
    extern char *progname;

#ifdef KEY_CHECK
   fprintf(stderr,"%s: checking keywords\n",progname);
   while(ptr->length != 0)
     {
        if(strlen(ptr->name) != ptr->length)
      {
        fprintf(stderr,
               "keyword %s, length is %d should be %d\n",
               ptr->name, strlen(ptr->name),
               ptr->length);
      }
        ptr++;
     }
   fprintf(stderr,"%s: done checking keywords,ok\n",
           progname);
   ptr = keywords;
```

```
#endif /* KEY_CHECK */

    while(ptr->length != 0)
        if(len == ptr->length &&
            (strcmp(ptr->name,string) == 0))
            {
#ifdef DEBUG
        fprintf(stderr,"%s: returning keyword # %d\n",
                progname, ptr->value);
#endif
        return ptr->value;
        }
    else
        {
#ifdef DEBUG
        fprintf(stderr,"%s: %s (%d) != %s (%d)\n",
                progname,ptr->name, ptr->length,
                string,len);
#endif
        ptr++;
        }

    return 0; /* no match */
}
```

Now that we have a reasonable lex specification, we must develop the yacc-driven parser. In the next section, we will take the grammar we developed in the previous chapter and convert that to a workable yacc grammar. Once our lexical analyzer and the yacc parser are completed, we have a complete skeleton from which the SGL is built.

Using Yacc to Implement SGL

Now that we have the lexical analyzer, we turn our attention to developing the yacc-driven parser. The grammar of the SGL is shown below (ε indicates an empty definition).

> *screen* ← **screen** **id** *screen_contents* **end** **id**
> *screen_contents* ← *type_list title regions*
> *type_list* ← *type_list type*
> *type* ← ε | **type** **id** **id**
> *title* ← **title** *title_lines* **end**
> *title_lines* ← *title_lines title_line*
> *title_line* ← ε | **title** **qstring**
> *regions* ← *regions region*
> *region* ← ε | **region** **id** *fields* **end** **id**

fields ← *field fields*
field ← ε | **field id type id** *bounds size*
bounds ← *lower_bound upper_bound*
lower_bound ← ε | **lower bound qstring**
upper_bound ← ε | **upper bound qstring**
size ← ε | **size integer**

As with lex, we first lay out our declarations. Since this will be our first revision, we are constructing the grammar to be clear and simple—this will make later work and refinement much easier! Indeed, it would be more surprising if we found our initial implementation was exactly correct. Nevertheless, we need a basis from which to work. First, we will need several terminals. For real numbers:

```
%token REAL
```

For integer numbers:

```
%token INTEGER
```

As with the MGL, we will have several types of alphanumeric characters: quoted strings, identifiers, and comments. As we mentioned in the lex section, we might also wish to have preprocessor commands. Thus, we have:

```
%token QSTRING ID COMMENT
```

Since we are not including preprocessor commands, we will not include a definition for them.

Finally, we get to the specific data types which truly define the SGL. The *keywords* used by the SGL (as we described in the previous chapter) yield:

```
%token SCREEN TYPE TITLE REGION
%token FIELD LOWER UPPER BOUND SIZE END
```

Recall that we can split the tokens up among as many lines as seems appropriate. Now that we have these terminals, we need to define the yacc union. Clearly, we need a separate type for **REAL** and similarly for **INTEGER**. All our string types are character pointers; all our commands are simply integers (but not of the same *semantic* value as a true integer). So we propose the following union definition:

```
%union {
    double  real;       /* real number */
    int     integer;    /* integer */
    char    *string;    /* string buffer */
    int     cmd;        /* command value */
}
```

The first three fields are relatively straightforward, but the fourth is merely a repetition of the second. We choose to include this repetitious field for program readability. When we access an *integer*, we will use the integer field, and when we wish to access the *command*, we will use the command field. This separation is based upon their *semantic* differences. Now we add the appropriate type declarations to our earlier token declarations. We now have:

```
%token <real> REAL
%token <integer> INTEGER
%token <string> QSTRING ID COMMENT
%token <cmd> SCREEN TYPE TITLE REGION
%token <cmd> FIELD LOWER UPPER BOUND SIZE END
```

With the declarations section complete, we turn our attention to the rules section. Logically, an SGL specification consists of a list of screens. Each screen constitutes an independent entity, so we first concentrate on the rule for a screen. We propose the following yacc rule:

```
screen:        SCREEN ID screen_contents END ID
               ;
```

For a single screen file, we will not require the user to provide a screen name. With this modification, we rewrite the rule:

```
screen:        screen_begin screen_contents screen_end

screen_begin:  SCREEN ID
             | SCREEN
               ;

screen_end:    END ID
             | END
               ;
```

It will be the responsibility of the user (and the C support routines) to assure that the **end** statement's screen name corresponds with the **screen** statement's name. Once we see these statements, we will call the C support routine that will set up the appropriate state. This is done, as before, with an appropriate *action*. Here are the actions we used:

```
screen:        screen_begin screen_contents screen_end

screen_begin:  SCREEN ID
                       { start_screen($2); }
             | SCREEN
                       { start_screen("default"); }
               ;
```

```
screen_end:     END ID
                        { end_screen($2); }
                | END
                        { end_screen("default"); }
                ;
```

Note the similarity to the earlier actions of the MGL. Indeed, we will see this pattern repeated several times, as screens are made up of individual components with similar syntactic rules.

Now we must develop the **screen_contents** rule. Here is our expansion of this rule:

```
screen_contents:    type_list title regions
                ;

type_list:          /* nothing */
                | TYPE ID type_list
                ;

title:              TITLE title_lines END
                ;

title_lines:        /* nothing */
                | title_lines TITLE QSTRING
                ;

regions:            region
                | regions region
                ;

region:     REGION ID fields END ID
        | REGION fields END
        ;
```

Although there is a great deal of similarity between each piece of the screen, we want to call your attention to one significant difference: the rule for **title_lines** allows zero or more title lines, while the rule for **region** does not. An alternative way of providing for no title would also be to change the **screen_contents** rule to read:

```
screen_contents:    type_list regions
                | type_list title regions
                ;
```

or to change the title definition:

```
title:              /* nothing */
                | TITLE title_lines END
                ;
```

Before using one of these forms, however, we would examine their effects more carefully, since the **type_list** rule also has an empty field, yielding an ambiguous grammar. Further examination of the **type_list** rule should indicate it is a straightforward, left-recursive rule. Although right-recursive rules can be used in yacc, left-recursive rules are preferred and, in general, generate more efficient parsers.

Each **region** is made up of a list of fields. The field is, in turn, made up of its own components. Here is our version of the **fields** rule and its subrules:

```
fields:         field
              | fields field
              ;

field:          FIELD ID TYPE ID bounds size
              ;

bounds:         lower_bound upper_bound
              ;

lower_bound:    /* nothing */
              | LOWER BOUND QSTRING
              ;

upper_bound:    /* nothing */
              | UPPER BOUND QSTRING
              ;

size:           /* nothing */
              | SIZE INTEGER
              ;
```

Note that, once again, the **fields** rule does not allow an empty list of rules (the programmer *must* have one field). Also, it is left-recursive, as were the previous rules. Recall the MGL's title line rule:

```
title:              title title
                  | TITLE QSTRING { add_title($2); }
                  ;
```

This type of rule leads to ambiguous grammars (although with yacc, they *do* work correctly). For example, suppose the input has three title lines. Because of this definition, the parser could either shift the first two rules or reduce them. In this particular case, it was unimportant, but we have structured the SGL so that no such ambiguities are present.

Our resultant yacc grammar is *not* the only possible description of this language. We have chosen this one because it is straightforward and has few reductions per rule, making modification, reading, and debugging much simpler.

We now must take our initial set of rules and expand the actions. Earlier we demonstrated the actions for the beginning and end of a screen; we will use a similar style to develop the actions used by the remainder of the grammar. Here are our proposed actions for the remaining sections of the grammar:

```
screen_contents:    type_list title regions
                 ;

type_list:          /* nothing */
                       { $$ = EMPTY; }
                 | type_list TYPE ID
                       {
                           install_type($3);
                           $$ = TYPE;
                       }
                 ;

title:              TITLE
                       { begin_title(); }
                    title_lines END
                       { end_title(); }
                 ;

title_lines:        /* nothing */
                       { warning("empty title section",
                         (char *)0); }
                 | title_lines TITLE QSTRING
                       { title_line($3); }
                 ;

regions:            region
                 | regions region
                 ;

region:             REGION ID
                       { start_region($2); }
                    fields END ID
                       { end_region($6); }
                 | REGION
                       { start_region("default"); }
                    fields END
                       { end_region("default"); }
                 ;

fields:             field
                 | fields field
                 ;

field:              FIELD ID TYPE ID lower_bound
                       upper_bound size
                       {
                           add_field($2,$4,$5,$6,$7);
```

```
                              }
                      ;

    lower_bound:          /* nothing */
                          { $$ = (char *)0; }
                        | LOWER BOUND QSTRING
                          { $$ = $3; }
                      ;

    upper_bound:          /* nothing */
                          { $$ = (char *)0; }
                        | UPPER BOUND QSTRING
                          { $$ = $3; }
                      ;

    size:                 /* nothing */
                          { $$ = default_size(type_str); }
                        | SIZE INTEGER
                          { int i;
                            sscanf($2,"%d",&i);
                            $$ = i;
                          }
                      ;
    %%

    #include "lex.yy.c"
```

The **screen_contents** rule is only an intermediate rule. It does not have any actions associated with it and is used only to further divide the underlying rules. The **type_list** rule demonstrates the functionality of *installable types*. An excellent way of dealing with installed types is to install the standard types. This allows all types, both initially defined and user-defined, to be identical in accessibility.

The **title** rule splits the actions over the rule itself. It calls **begin_title**, then processes the actual title lines, finishing with the call to **end_title**. The begin/end routines should generate any necessary pre- and postamble code necessary, as well as set up any desired state. The title's primary contents are described by the **title_lines** rule. Each line consists of the keyword **title** and a quoted string. The **title_line** routine is called with the value of the quoted string.

Next the **regions** rule is another intermediate rule. Individual regions are made up of another begin/end pair (the **region** keyword and the **end** keyword). As with **title_lines**, the rule is split to allow pre- and post-processing around the component fields. The **fields** rule consists of a list of individual **field** rules which are the fundamental unit of work in screen generation. After matching the various arguments (through the **lower_bound**, **upper_bound**, and **size** rules), the routine **add_field** is called. This routine either generates the necessary code or saves sufficient information so the screen generator can actually develop the final code for the screen region.

Recall that we used dynamic allocation in our lexical analyzer. If we had not done this, the above program would have become far more complex. For example, the **field** rule uses several quoted strings. If each of these strings was lost the next time **yylex** was called (which it would be), we would be forced to save the data away—either in global buffers or in dynamically allocated buffers. By performing this dynamic allocation in the lexical analyzer rather than in the parser, we also minimize the number of points where memory is dynamically allocated.

We now have completed the first two parts of the SGL. However, the third portion consists of a large number of support routines. Because our goal was to demonstrate using lex and yacc, we will leave it to the reader to actually implement these routines. We have little doubt that as the SGL undergoes use, it will need further refinement. However, the basic principles set forth here should work when refining the language and adding additional features.

Intermediate Languages

It might seem to some readers that because all our compiler examples use an intermediate language, this is the only way lex and yacc can be used. We wish to stress that this is, in fact, not true. Certainly, since lex and yacc are UNIX tools, they are often used to generate C as an intermediate language. This is, however, a product of the environment in which they are used.

Using No Intermediate Language

There is, indeed, no requirement that lex or yacc generate *any* intermediate language. For instance, we developed a simple desktop calculator whose only output was the result of the computation. In that case, yacc was used to build an *interpreter*. An intermediate language is usually used when creating a *compiler*, such as the MGL or SGL, or a more traditional compiler, such as a C compiler.

An excellent example of a compiler without an intermediate language would be a text formatter, such as *troff*, the UNIX text formatter. The output is sent directly to the printer.* Other examples abound; an assembler is an example of just such a compiler.

---

*Of course, it could be argued that the printer's language is, in fact, an intermediate language.

Using an Intermediate Language

Lex and yacc were used in the SGL and MGL cases to implement higher-level programming functions in terms of the lower-level constructs of C, although we could have used *any intermediate* language. Indeed, this is a commonly used approach—so-called fourth-generation languages (4GLs) are often compilers, much like the SGL or MGL, which compile into a lower-level language which is then executed by the 4GLs' run-time module.

Another advantage of using the higher-level language approach is portability. The C language provides a model of an abstract machine which the programmer is manipulating. It is the compiler that, in turn, implements the C program in the *real* machine where the program must run. If the abstract machine is general enough, it is often unnecessary to rewrite the program when compiling on a new real machine. Of course, like any abstraction, it may limit your ability to use some specific hardware feature. The UNIX operating system consists of many lines of C code, yet a small portion of the underlying code is assembler—specifically to short-circuit the abstraction offered by C. This would include such functions as implementing special machine instructions (e.g., **mfpr** on a VAX or **trap** on a SUN) or manipulating hardware. The tradeoff is in portability—an assembly language program for a VAX will most likely not work for a SUN.

The SGL began as a language description that made no assumptions of the underlying language. It should be possible, then, by implementing the appropriate support routines and changing the lexical analyzer to recognize the new language's identifiers and generate code in a language besides C, for example, Modula-2. Thus, the screen specification becomes independent of the intermediate language. If it must be ported amongst various environments, this portability can be an important feature. Further, if the predominant language changes from C to C++, the MGL and SGL can be rewritten to take advantage of the new features of C++ without changing the screen specifications. Thus, an application becomes less dependent upon the underlying environment—just as an application written for a UNIX machine is less dependent upon the hardware environment than an assembly-language-based program.

Using Nontraditional Languages

Finally, there is no requirement that the intermediate language be a traditional programming language (such as C, Pascal, FORTRAN, COBOL, Modula-2, or Post-Script). Instead the intermediate language could be a set of related data structures. Indeed, this is a routine technique for doing code compilation with just such traditional programming languages. A C compiler, for instance, often consists of a preprocessor, a syntactic compiler which generates symbol tables, a data flow pass which reads the symbol table generated by the first pass and creates a data flow diagram of the code. The third pass then reads the symbol table and the data flow diagram and performs code generation and optimization. The intermediate language then consists of these data structures.

The number of possible intermediate languages then is unlimited—it is more a function of the application's goals than of the application itself. An SGL user would be impartial if the program he (or she) wrote compiled to C or Modula-2, so long as the output performs the desired task correctly.

A Reference for
Lex Specifications

Declarations and Definitions Section
Rules Section
Code Section

In this chapter, we discuss the format of the lex specification and describe the various features and options available to the lex programmer. This chapter is intended to summarize the capabilities that we have demonstrated in the examples in previous chapters as well as cover some features that have not been discussed.

Lex is specifically designed to accept language descriptions as regular expressions and, from that description, to construct a finite automaton which accepts (or rejects) the language. A lex specification provides a simple-to-maintain description of the lexical analyzer. With the advent of newer lex tools (e.g., the GNU project's lex replacement, *flex*), the generated analyzers run very fast indeed.

It is interesting to compare a custom C-based lexical routine versus a lex specification. A C-based lexical routine is typically larger and more complex than the comparable lex description of an equivalent lexical analyzer. In Example 6-1, we demonstrate a C-based lexical analyzer of reasonable power and, in Example 6-2, a lex description of an equivalent lexical analyzer, similar to one used for the MGL project in Chapter 4, *The MGL*.

Example 6-1. Sample C-based lexical analyzer

```
#include <stdio.h>
#include <ctype.h>
char *progname;
int lineno = 1;
int Out_lineno = 1; /* output line number */

yylex()
{
    int c;

    while ((c=getchar()) == ' ' || c == '\t')
        ;
    if (c == EOF)
        return 0;
    if (c == '.' || isdigit(c)) {     /* number */
        ungetc(c, stdin);
        scanf("%lf", &yylval.val);
        return NUMBER;
    }
    if ( c == '#' ) { /* comment */
        char *p = textbuf;
        int index = 1;
        do {
                if (index < sizeof(textbuf)) *p++ = c;
        } while ((c = getchar()) != EOF && c != '\n');
        ungetc(c,stdin);
        yylval.text = textbuf;
        return COMMENT;
    }
    if ( c == '"' ) { /* literal text */
        char *p = textbuf;
        int index = 1;
        while ((c = getchar()) != EOF &&
                c != '"' && c != '\n' &&
                index < sizeof(textbuf))
        {
            *p++ = c;
        }
        *p = '\0';
        if(c == '\n') ungetc(c,stdin);
        yylval.text = textbuf;
        return TEXT;
    }

    if ( isalpha(c)) { /* check to see if it is a command */
        char *p = textbuf;
        int index = 1;

        do {
            *p++ = c;
        } while ((c = getchar()) != EOF && isalnum(c));
        ungetc(c, stdin);
```

Example 6-1. Sample C-based lexical analyzer (continued)

```
        *p = '\0';
        yylval.text = textbuf;
        return COMMAND;
    }
    if ( c == '\n') lineno++;
    return c;
}

yyerror(s) /* called for yacc syntax error */
char *s;
{
    warning(s, (char *)0);
}

warning(s, t)      /* print warning message */
char *s, *t;
{
    fprintf(stderr, "%s: %s", progname, s);
    if (t)
        fprintf(stderr, " %s", t);
    fprintf(stderr, " near line %\n", lineno);
}
```

Lex uses a three-part specification for generating the lexical analyzer. These sections are the declarations or definitions section, the rules section, and the code section. Lex generates a file named *lex.yy.c* that contains the C-code lexical analyzer routine **yylex**.

Example 6-2. Sample lex specification

```
%%
[ \t]+                          ;
[0-9]+                  |
[0-9]+\.[0-9]+          |
\.[0-9]+                        { sscanf(yytext, "&lf", &yylval.val);
                                  return NUMBER;
                                }
#*                              { yylval.text = yytext;
                                  return COMMENT;
                                }
\"[^\"\n]*\"                    { yylval.text = yytext;
                                  return TEXT;
                                }
[a-zA-Z][a-zA-Z0-9]+            { yylval.text = yytext;
                                  return COMMAND;
                                }
\n                              { lineno++; return '\n'; }
.                              { yylval.text = (char *)0;
                                  return yytext[0];
```

Example 6-2. Sample lex specification (continued)

```
                                  }
  %%
```

To create the lexical analyzer, you process the specification file using lex.

Declarations and Definitions Section

The lex declarations section consists of two parts. The first is the introduction of any C declarations that are used by the user-supplied C code. The second is the introduction of any definitions that are used by the lex specification in the second (rules) section. For simple lexical analyzers, this section might contain nothing.

When the lex output file (*lex.yy.c*) is not included in the yacc file,* we need symbols representing tokens. Yacc generates a header file named *y.tab.h* when we call it with the **-d** switch. Also, when using lex with yacc, we need to know the definition of the yacc union, so our actions (in the rules section) can return the data in the union. This information is also included in the yacc-generated header file. When *not* using yacc, the programmer is responsible for maintaining these definitions.

Preliminary code, such as **#include** lines, is incorporated into the lex specification (and subsequent lexical analyzer) by using the %{ ... %} code block. Here is an example which includes an external definition file for the tokens:

```
  %{
  #include "tokens.h"
  %}
```

This literal block may contain *any* valid C code.

---

*We might not include *lex.yy.c* for a large lexical analyzer or a large yacc parser to avoid recompilation of the parser due to changes in the lexical analyzer.

Definitions

In the lex specification samples we have shown so far, we rely upon *substitutions*. These are frequently used to mnemonically define regular expressions employed in the rules section. An example of such a substitution might be:

```
digit [0-9]
```

This definition is then referenced by placing braces ({ }) around the desired substitution string. For example, the *digit* definition could be then used to define a real number:*

```
{digit}+|{digit}*.{digit}+
```

Start States

We also declare *start states* in the declarations section. Start states are used to limit the scope of certain rules. The processing of a *preprocessor directive* illustrates one use of start states. For example, in a C preprocessor directive, some interpretations are no longer valid. Suppose we have the following C preprocessor directive:

```
#include "./*.h"
```

Normally, the sequence "/*" indicates the beginning of a C comment, but in this case, that meaning is *not* valid. A start rule can then be used to indicate a set of rules to be applied only when lex is in a certain state. However, be warned that those rules that do *not* have start rules are exercised in *any* state!†

A *start rule* is declared by using the %s declaration. For example:

```
%s PREPROC
```

would indicate that lex should expect to see the state **PREPROC**. In the rules section, then, a rule that has <PREPROC> prepended to it will *only* apply in state **PREPROC**.

Keep in mind that the "+" and "" of these examples are not used in their typical arithmetic sense. Rather, they are used as regular expression operators.

†Indeed, this is a singularly common lex programming mistake. Take note, however, because the GNU project's replacement, *flex*, does *not* follow this convention. See Appendix D, *GNU Flex*, for further information regarding *flex*.

Changing Internal Tables

Lex uses internal tables of a fixed size, although it does allow the programmer to increase the size of the tables themselves. Following is a set of declarations associated with lex's table sizes.

%a Increase the action optimization table.

%e Increase the size of the parse tree.

%k Increase the number of packed character classes.

%n Increase the number of possible states.

%o Increase the output array size.

%p Increase the number of possible positions.

To find out what the current statistics are, call lex with the -v flag. For example, the sample grammar (shown in Example 6-2) used 55 of 1000 tree nodes (%e), 113/2500 positions (%p), 19/500 states (%n), 698/2000 transitions (%a), 26/1000 packed character classes (%k), and 167/3000 output slots (%o). Clearly, it takes a significantly larger grammar to fill the default size of the tables. Further, it is possible to construct regular expressions that will lead to very large machines. In general, it is better to simplify these expressions by either writing them in a simpler form, splitting them into multiple expressions, or writing C code to handle more of the work.

Except for large projects, it will not be necessary to increase the table sizes. To figure out optimal sizes for the tables, the programmer should significantly increase the various values and then run lex with the -v flag, finally adjusting those internal values closer to the actual needs of the lexical analyzer.

Character Translations

Lex makes certain presumptions about the meanings of the input tokens as characters. The most significant presumption can be that each character is distinct and the codes should be interpreted as ASCII characters. This would not be true, for example, for writing a utility to convert from EBCDIC to ASCII. Lex allows the programmer to modify these assumptions by building a *translation table* with the %T directive. Additionally, the three internal lex routines, **input, output,** and **unput,*** must also be modified to understand the new mapping conventions. These input and output routines are initially macros; to replace them, an

---

***input** is used to obtain another character from the input stream, **output** is used to place a character on the output stream, and **unput** is used to push a character back onto the input stream—thus allowing for lookahead.

#undefine should be done in this initial section by embedding them inside a %% pair.

To demonstrate the use of the **%T** directive, we can show a sample conversion which maps the upper- and lower-case letters to the values 1 through 26, the digits 0 through 9 to the values 27 through 36, newline to 37, "+" to 38, and "-" to 39. Our sample declaration is shown in Figure 6-1.

```
%T
1        aA
2        bB
3        cC
.
.
.
26       zZ
27       0
28       1
.
.
.
36       9
37       \n
38       +
39       -
%T
```

Figure 6-1. Sample lex translation table

Actual use of this capability is typically restricted to specialized applications.

Rules Section

The second section of the lex specification consists of the *rules section*. It is this section which actually defines the functionality of the lexical analyzer and, in some sense, does all the work within lex. Each rule consists of a regular expression and an associated action.

UNIX Regular Expression Syntax

A *regular expression* is a specific mathematical object. A mathematical regular expression can consist of nothing (the empty set), any single character, the union or concatenation of any two regular expressions, or the repetition of a regular expression. Lex regular expressions are nearly identical to those used by the UNIX editor, *ed*. This format for writing regular expressions allows them to be written concisely.

Many programs besides lex use these regular expressions, so understanding them is generally useful. Now we will discuss the regular expressions from Example 6-2. The first pattern:

```
[ \t]+
```

consists of two parts. The first part is:

```
[ \t]
```

which by itself matches exactly two strings: the string consisting of a single space, and the string consisting of a single tab. The second part, "+", operates on the first part by allowing any nonempty combination of tabs and spaces. More specifically, the "+" denotes the concatenation of one or more of the specified symbols. All this rule is doing, then, is stripping out "whitespace" characters. Note that the action after this rule is *empty*. Nothing is done with whitespace.

The second pattern is:

```
[0-9]+           |
[0-9]+\.[0-9]+ |
\.[0-9]+
```

As before, this pattern uses the *concatenation* operator (+), but it also uses the union operator (I). This allows the description of the regular expression as a *choice* among the three types specified. The backslash (\) before the dot (.) is an *escape* character, denoting that the following character should be interpreted literally rather than given any special meaning (a dot is a *wildcard*, representing any single ASCII character).

This definition is an attempt to describe a *number*. It states that it must be one of three possibilities:

- A series of digits.
- A series of digits, a decimal point, and a second series of digits.
- A decimal point followed by a series of digits.

Of course, this part of the specification will generate a lexical routine that does not work the same as the one in Example 6-1; the previous version considered "." to be a number, the latter does not.

There are several special characters, such as "+", "|", and ".". A full list is contained in Table 6-1, along with a brief explanation of the operation of each one. Any of the special characters can be used in a regular expression by preceding it with a "\". To get a "\", you need only type "\\".

Table 6-1: Lex Regular Expressions Operators

Character	Meaning
.	Matches any single character (except newline).
$	Matches the end of the line.
^	Matches beginning of line, except inside [] when it means "complement".
[ ]	Matches any of the specified characters.
-	Inside [], if it is not the first character, means "the range of".
?	The previous regular expression is optional (e.g., 10?9 is 109 or 19).
*	Any number of repetitions, including zero.
+	Any positive number of repetitions, but not zero.
|	Allows alternation between two expressions (e.g., 10|11 matches 10 or 11).
( )	Allows grouping of expressions.
/	Matches an expression if followed by the next expressions (e.g., 10/11 matches 10 11).
{ }	Allows repetitions or substitutes a definition.
< >	Defines a start condition.

Although the regular expressions we have demonstrated are powerful, we have not yet delved into any of the more complex regular expression operators. In general, we have found that most regular expressions can be written using the simpler format. Occasionally, however, it becomes necessary to use more subtle operations, so we will describe them all in detail. First, the operators used to describe UNIX regular expressions are:

```
[] - ? . * + | () {} ^
```

The operators:

```
" \ %
```

are not part of the regular expression; rather they are used by lex itself for control. For example, "\n" is used to denote the *newline character* (similarly, "\t" denotes a tab, etc.). For characters with a special meaning, "\" is used to remove that meaning. The special character ' " ' is used to denote the beginning (and end) of a string literal. Finally, " % " is used to denote special regions within the lex specification file. The special characters are described in Table 6-2.

Table 6-2: Control Characters in Lex Specifications

Character	Meaning
\	Escapes the following character (removes "magic" meaning). Also used to represent nonprintable characters, such as "\n" (newline).
"	Accepts the input string until the next " is seen. If a newline is found, there is an error.
%	Used by lex in the declarations section to separate source segments.

The operators ^$/<> are used to circumvent the constraints of regular expressions by allowing matching of context-sensitive tokens.

The first set of operators:

```
[]-?.*+|(){} and ^ inside [].
```

simplify the writing of regular expressions. Brackets ([]) provide a simple mechanism for providing choices between various characters. Although we can describe the same regular expression using different operators, we can often write the expression in a very compact form. For instance, the first expression for matching a number, "[0-9]+", could be rewritten as:

```
(0|1|2|3|4|5|6|7|8|9)+
```

Although this means the same thing, it is more awkward. The "-" operator can have its usual meaning, minus, or it can mean "the range of," as it does in the "[0-9]+" expression. Once again, it does not change the expression; it only makes writing the expression simpler. The "?" operator allows for simplifying regular expressions with (possibly) other expressions inside. For instance, it is possible to match C-like expressions such as "if" and "ifdef" with such a (single) rule: "if(def)?". As mentioned before, the "." matches any character. Clearly, each character could be specified by using the bracket operators ([]); the characters could be explicitly written, but this is a much simpler way of writing a comparable regular expression. The "*" and "+" operators are repetition operators. After a regular expression, say, "[0-9]", "*" would mean zero or more times, while "+" would mean one or more times. Thus, "*" allows the specified regular expression to "vanish", while the "+" requires at least one occurrence of the string. For the sample, it would be possible to rewrite the recognition of decimal numbers, changing it from:

```
[0-9]+\.[0-9]+|\.[0-9]+
```

to:

```
[0-9]*\.[0-9]+
```

The resultant machine works no differently.

The "|" has been used without a clear definition, but it should be simple for the experienced UNIX programmer to guess that it means "or". Specifically, it is the *alternation* operator. Note that in the sample program, a number is defined as:

```
[0-9]+|[0-9]+\.[0-9]+|\.[0-9]+
```

The "|" operator implies that a number can be any one of the three forms. The parentheses, (), are useful to group an expression. This can be especially important when using the "+", "*", or "?" operators. Notice that in the "if(def)?" example, grouping was used to construct the regular expression. Without parentheses, this expression would have been:

```
if|ifdef
```

Finally, in the case of braces ({}), they can be used as a specific repetition operator. For instance, the expression:

```
if(def)\{0,1}
```

is equivalent to "if(def)?", as it allows def to be repeated zero or one times.

Finally, using these more compact operators, we condense our previous declaration of a number:

```
{digit}*(.{digit}+)?
```

which uses more of these "simplifying" techniques than the original version of the expression did. This expression is not nearly as easily read without a full understanding of the lex regular expression operators.

Finally, there is the caret (^), which is used inside brackets ([]) for *complementation*. That is, rather than matching the specified character or characters, it matches everything *but* the specified character. For example, here is a regular expression which finds a quoted string:

```
\"[^\"\n]*\"
```

Initially, it might not be clear to the reader why we do not use the simpler form:

```
\"*[\n\"]
```

Alas, because lex tries to match as much text as possible, it will use the wildcard (*) to match as much text as possible. If we were analyzing the C line:

```
strcmp("foo","bar");
```

this simpler expression would group everything between the initial parenthesis, (, and the final parenthesis,), as a single string. Thus, the parser would be handed the token **foo","bar**—not the the desired result.

There are cases when it is necessary to deal with expressions that cannot be described as regular expressions. These are expressions which require knowledge of the context in which they are invoked. For instance, nested comments cannot be detected by a regular expression.* However, it is often possible to get around some of these difficulties by adding a context-determination mechanism. That is the purpose of the third set of operators: ^$/<>. First, the "^" operator specifies a left-context sensitivity—left in the sense that the beginning of the line occurred previously in the input stream. An excellent example of this is that rules of interpretation change when processing a preprocessor statement in C. For instance, suppose the following preprocessor statement is seen inside a C file:

```
#include "sys/*foo.h"
```

The "*" looks like the beginning of a comment. But, in this case, this is not true. The "^" can be used to detect that a preprocessor statement is being examined. For instance, this could be done by introducing a flag, as in the following example:

---

*Intuitively, this problem requires counting, a task which finite automata are not capable of doing. Such problems are handled by *pushdown automata*, a form of finite automaton; pushdown automata are the model of automata used by yacc. A formal argument uses the pumping lemma for regular sets. If L is the language of all nested comments, $L = \{x | x = /*(/**/)* * /\}$, then it can be shown that L is not regular. First, for any n, choose a string $z \in L$ so that $|z| \geq 4n$. Now by the pumping lemma (for regular sets), $z = uvw$, where $|uv| \leq n$, $|v| \geq 1$. Now it is clear that uv^2iw is not in L if $i \neq 1$, since we are pumping only the opening side of the comments, not the closing side of the comments (and, hence, they do not match up).

```
int preproc = 0;
%%
^# { preproc = 1; ECHO; }
\n { preproc = 0; ECHO; }
/* additional rules */
```

Then the appropriate routines can be written to check for that flag. Another way to accomplish the same thing is to provide a *starting state* for some (or all) of the states. First, the start states must be listed in the declarations section using the %start keyword. Then to enter a particular start condition, the action associated with the rule has a **BEGIN** <state> statement. Rules specific to that start condition should have the start state at the head of the rule. The above example could thus become:

```
\%start PREPROC
%%
^#          { ECHO; BEGIN PREPROC; }
\n          { ECHO; BEGIN 0; }
<PREPROC>" { /* ... */ }
/* additional rules */
```

In general, a rule without a start state is valid for *any* state. Thus, this rule must be carefully used.

Right context sensitivity is controlled by the "$" and "/". The "$" represents a newline (\n). The "/" is used to match a string if it is followed by a particular string. For instance, a sample language where END may be followed by "." or ";" or nothing depending on whether it terminated a code block, a statement block, or neither. Upon seeing each type of END, the compiler must check to determine if it is, indeed, the correct end, so it is important to determine what the type actually is. This sample grammar illustrates the use of "/" to match correctly:

```
%%
END/.    { ECHO; } /* check code block termination */
END/;    { ECHO; } /* check statement block termination */
END      { ECHO; } /* check other condition(s) */
```

Clearly, this case could have been written to directly match "END.", "END;", and "END". The yacc grammar would have been different from this result, however. Recall that for the rule **x/y, x** matches if and only if it is followed by **y. y** is *not* removed from the input stream.

Variables

yyleng

The lex variable **yyleng** identifies the number of characters which matched the regular expression. For instance, if the token **froboz** matched a regular expression such as "[a-zA-Z][0-9a-zA-Z]*" (the regular expression we used for identifiers), **yyleng** would be six. Thus, the last character of this token could be referenced as "yytext[yyleng-1]".

yytext

Lex stores the matched token into the **yytext** character array. C routines may access this variable, which is a single global variable, as if it were any other normal character array.

Macros

BEGIN

This macro places lex in a state. Rules beginning with the specified state are now activated (as well as any unrestricted states).

ECHO

This macro prints the current token to the output. It is equivalent to "printf(" %s",yytext)".

REJECT

This macro continues to try to match against other actions. Without a **REJECT**, the first match will be the only one acted upon. With a **REJECT**, it is possible to have multiple matches for the same token.

input

Lex uses the macro **input** to obtain the next character from the input stream. Although this generally is sufficient (as the input stream can be redirected with the **freopen** library call from the *stdio* library), it cannot handle some special cases. In this case, the compiler writer can rewrite the **input** macro to provide the required functionality. Note that because of the use of **unput**, any **input** macro must be able to handle characters that are examined and then pushed back to the head of the input stream. This is done simply in a system buffering such input. One special case necessitating rewriting **input** is when processing a binary file.

output

Lex uses this macro to write out any input it has. As with **input**, this can be rewritten for those special cases where the standard **output** routine cannot be used.

unput

This routine is used to perform lookahead where the next character is, in fact, not needed. Because this cannot be determined until after the character has been read with **input**, **unput** is used to push the unwanted character back onto the front of the input stream. Typically, this will have to be rewritten whenever **input** is rewritten.

Routines

yyless

This routine is used to place tokens back on the stack. For instance, if an expression is ambiguous, the action could choose to take one possible form of the expression and push the excess characters back into the input stream. An example of this is the *pcc* compiler's handling of an expression such as:

```
b =-a;
```

which lex recognizes as "b", "=-", and "a". The action routines, upon seeing the "=-", warn that this is an ambiguous assignment (this was an older form of the "-=" operator) and push the "-" sign back into the input stream, giving the same effect as if the expression had been written:

```
b = -a;
```

The routine **yyless** takes a single argument—the number of characters to push back into the input stream.

yymore

This routine is used to request that lex continue processing without overwriting the existing contents of **yytext**. The most predominant use of this is to process continuation lines, such as the following:

```
"this is a line of \
text"
```

When the higher-level routine sees the "\" it calls **yymore** to obtain the balance of the token. Then **yytext** will contain:

```
"this is a line of text"
```

yyreject

This is the code which implements the **REJECT** macro. The actual routine is provided in the lex library *libl.a*.

yywrap

This routine is used to handle end-of-file conditions gracefully. If there is more input to process, **yywrap** returns 0; otherwise, it returns 1. Its most useful purpose is in providing end-of-file statistics; it can also be used to open a new input source and continue normal processing. For example, it may be necessary to allow inclusions of some postamble file using the same syntax. This routine, when called, could be responsible for attaching to that stream.

The default code for **yywrap** is typically something like:

```
yywrap { return 1; }
```

For lex, it is included in the lex library *libl.a* and is included transparently. To replace this routine, the compiler writer need merely insert a custom **yywrap** routine in one of the compiler source files; when linking, the file containing **yywrap** must come before *libl.a* on the command line.

Code Section

The final section of a lex specification is the code section. This section may contain any valid C code. Typically, it will contain supporting routines for the lex actions. Frequently, this section will have no code, as the necessary routines will be provided by the lex library.

Including Code

In addition to placing code directly in the code section, there are two other ways to place code in a specification:

1. Any lines beginning with a blank or a tab are not interpreted by lex and are copied as C code into *lex.yy.c*.

   - If the code appears before the first %%, it will be external to any function in the code.

   - If it appears after the first %%, it will be local to the **yylex** function.

2. Any C code placed between lines containing only the delimiters %{ and %} will be copied out to *lex.yy.c* as is. While this method can be used to include code anywhere in the specification, it typically appears in the definitions section to accommodate preprocessor statements. For instance, you might see:

   ```
   %{
   #include <math.h>
   %}
   ```

7

A Reference for Yacc Specifications

Declarations Section
Rules Section
Code Section

This chapter provides a detailed description of yacc, referencing the full range of features available to the experienced programmer.

As with lex, we first divide our discussion of yacc into describing the three parts of the yacc specification. We conclude this chapter with a discussion of continuation processing.

In our discussion of the yacc file, we will use the simple model grammar shown in Example 7-1. This sample program was designed to read the input and, when it matched a string, print "string" and, when it matched a number, print "number". If it does not recognize the text as either a string or a number, it will print an error message.

Example 7-1. Sample yacc program listing

```
%{
char textbuf[100];
%}
%union {
    int     cmd;        /* command */
    char    *text;      /* text */
    double  val;        /* value */
}
%token    <text>      TEXT COMMENT
%token    <val>       NUMBER
%token    <cmd>       COMMAND

%start list

%%
list:       object
          | list object
          | error '\n' { warning("unknown object",(char *)0); }
          ;

object:     string      { printf("string\n"); }
          | number      { printf("number\n"); }
          | '\n'
          ;

string:     TEXT
          | COMMENT
          | COMMAND
          ;

number:     NUMBER
          | '+' NUMBER
          | '-' NUMBER
          | NUMBER '.' NUMBER
          ;

%%
#include "progs.c"
```

Declarations Section

The first section, the declarations section, contains declarations that must be known throughout the entire parser. As with lex, this section is used for both C declarations for the code used in the actions (described in "Rules Section" below) as well as declarations needed by yacc.

The purpose of the declarations section is to establish the framework of the parser; the tokens and operators to be used, as well as their characteristics, are defined. The form of the token is declared, in addition to any global variables that will be used. At the end of this section, there is a terminator, the double percent (%%) on a line by itself.

C Declarations

In the sample yacc file (shown in Example 7-1), the C declarations section includes a declaration of the buffer **textbuf**. In general, the contents of the %{ and }% (a *literal block*) can be any valid C code. By convention, it is used only for variable and function declarations, includes, and macros, since code can be placed in the code section (see "Code Section" below). The literal block is copied exactly into the front of the yacc output file. Thus, when examining the yacc output, the declaration of **textbuf** will be at the beginning of the file.

Union Declarations

Yacc deals with a fundamental type known as a *token*. Because this token can take several different forms, yacc allows the program specification to define a C **union** that corresponds to all possible forms the token might take:

```
%union {
    int     cmd;     /* command */
    char   *text;    /* text */
    double  val;     /* value */
}
```

In this particular example, a token can be either a *command*, a *text* string, or an integer *value*. In the absence of the %**union** declaration, the default is to use an integer. For many simpler grammars, this often will suffice. For instance, in this example, an integer would have been sufficient. However, we used the more complex form as a demonstration of its use. Use of the **union** enhances portability; it also makes the operation of the parser clearer to another person.

Token Type Declarations

Token definitions describe all possible tokens that the lexical analyzer will return to the parser. A token is the atomic unit upon which the parser operates. It can be a single character, a digit, an entire number, a string, or any other recognizable unit. For instance, the keywords of a language are the principal set of tokens with which a parser is concerned; they might be referred to as **KEYWORD** in the token section or, in this case, as the more general **COMMAND**. It depends upon the grammar, and the implementation of the grammar, as to what the use of tokens will be. A token declaration, then, consists of the keyword **%token** followed by, in angle brackets (<>), the element of the union corresponding to the token or tokens and then the name (or names) of the tokens themselves. The tokens can be grouped or listed separately on each line. So, the example could have read:

```
%token <text> TEXT
%token <val> NUMBER
%token <text> COMMENT
%token <cmd> COMMAND
```

instead of the order used in the example. Note that if we do not use **%union**, the element declaration can be foregone. Thus, if we did not use it in the above example, our **%token** line could have been:

```
%token TEXT NUMBER COMMENT COMMAND
```

While yacc *will* allow you to leave out the token type declaration, it requires anyone reading the program after you to understand an obscure yacc assumption. Better to keep it clean and always spell out what the type of a token is.

Nonterminal Type Declarations

The **%type** declaration is used when a **%union** declaration has defined multiple token types. Just as **%token** defines the token type, **%type** defines the type of nonterminal symbols. You do not need to associate a type with a nonterminal symbol if it does not assign a token value ("$$") in its action. That is why our sample specification does not have this declaration.

Start Declarations

The **%start** declaration defines which rule is the top-level rule; that is, the rule that the parser will begin to use first. If this declaration is omitted, the parser begins by using the first rule in the rules section. It is, however, a good idea to list explicitly the first rule in this section; experimental grammars have a habit of growing quickly, and the simple action of listing the starting spot will help you and anyone else who reads the code to follow the flow of control more readily.

Precedence

None of the declarations in the example demonstrates *precedence* or *associativity*. A common problem when building a parser is the order in which a string of tokens is *reduced* into a *parse tree*. It is this parse tree that allows the yacc-generated parser to perform the correct actions. Thus, it is often desirable to define the precedence of a particular operator. An excellent example are the basic mathematical operations "+", "-", "*", and "/". *A priori* there is no reason that an arithmetic expression, say, "3 * 4 + 6 / 2", must be interpreted as is taught in school. The sample could then provide several different answers, depending upon how it is interpreted; in this case, the correct answer could be 9, 15, or 21.†
Thus, to avoid ambiguity, it is necessary to define the *order* in which operations should be performed. The traditional way to define these operations would correspond with the following yacc declaration:

```
%left '+' '-'
%left '*' '/'
```

The **%left** declares the operators to be left-associative, while the order in which they are declared fixes their precedence, from least binding to most binding. Thus, with the previous example, "+" and "-" are of equal precedence and are both left-associative, while "*" and "/", still being left-associative, are of higher precedence than "+" and "-".

In addition to left associativity (**%left**), there is also right associativity (**%right**) and nonassociativity (**%nonassoc**). An example of a right-associative operator is the "=" sign in a C program. An example of a nonassociative operator is the closure operator.

Associativity can be thought of as answering the question: which side of the expressions should be simplified first? For the left-associative operator, it would be the expression on the left ("2 + 3 + 4" would be viewed as "(2 + 3) + 4"). For the right-associative operator, it would be the expression on the right ("x = y / 14" would be interpreted as "x = (y / 14)"). For the nonassociative operator, to find two in a row would be an error (a** is exactly the same as a*, so the extra closure operator is meaningless).

---

†The possibilities are: $(((3*4)+6)/2)$, which equals 9; $(3*((4+6)/2))$, which equals 15; or $(3*(4+(6/2)))$, which equals 21.

The token names that appear in a precedence declaration are at the same time declared as tokens, making use of the **%token** declaration redundant. This declaration constitutes declaration of the appropriate tokens. For example, the line:

```
%left UNARYMINUS
```

could also have been listed, in which case an explicit declaration for the token **UNARYMINUS** would have been made. In the case of individual characters, the parser treats them as tokens already.*

Rules Section

After the declarations section, the rules section begins. This is the *heart* of the parser, whereas the declarations section was an area for housekeeping and accounting activities. It is the rules section that gives the yacc parser generator its power.

In the example, the first rule happens to be the starting rule; this does not have to be the case (i.e., it could be redefined by using the **%start** operator in the declarations section), but for this example, it is. The rule **list** is followed by a list of all possible token combinations that constitute a **list**. In this case, a **list** could be an **object**. Since **object** was not defined as a terminal, it must be a rule. Looking further into the rules section, the rule for **object** can be seen. Note that with **list**, the line where **object** was first seen does not have an *action* associated with *finding* an **object**.

In general, a *rule* consists of one or more token sets with an optional action for each token set. New token sets are formed by *concatenation*, or *union*, of token sets. For instance, in the case of the **list** rule, it consists of three token sets. An error followed by a newline constitutes a list. Finally, an *object* constitutes a valid list; a list followed by an object is also valid.

The remaining rules demonstrate that there are two types of "tokens". Initially, the difference between them is that one type is *declared* in the declarations section, while the second type is only used within the rules section. For instance, in the example, the tokens **list** and **object** are *not* declared in the declarations section, while the tokens **TEXT**, **COMMENT**, **STRING**, and **NUMBER** are. Aside from the obvious difference of punctuation (which is only a stylistic difference

---

*When yacc generates the parser, the "tokens" 0 through 256 are reserved, with 0 through 255 representing all possible eight-bit characters. The other tokens, then, are declared by symbolic constants whose numbering begins at 257. Thus, it is never necessary to declare explicitly any single character as a token; however, with the operators, it is still necessary to define their precedence and associativity.

ignored by yacc), they describe different types of objects. A **NUMBER**, for instance, is a single indivisible unit (well, we've *chosen* it to be one). Such a fundamental unit is a *terminal*. A compound rule is made up of terminals *and* compound rules. These compound rules are *nonterminals*. Yacc predefines some terminals for your convenience, notably all individual characters in which you might be interested.*

A literal character is enclosed in single quotes, such as '='. The backslash (\) has special meaning, as in C, being used for escape sequences. The following special character escape sequences are valid:

'\n'	newline
'\r'	return
'\''	single quote
'\\'	backslash
'\t'	tab
'\b'	backspace
'\f'	form feed
'\xxx'	character whose octal value is *xxx*

Error Token

The first rule in the sample grammar refers to a nonterminal symbol named **error**. However, there is *no* definition for **error**. Nor is there a token defined for it in the declarations section. The name, however, gives away its purpose—error handling. The **error** token is a specially defined yacc token that essentially means that any token that does not match one of the previous rules must match this rule. The token after the **error** token is a *synchronizing* character. In other words, yacc will throw away all tokens until it sees (in this case) a newline.

This allows the parser to perform a type of *error recovery*. When an error occurs, it is better to attempt recovery and continue processing the input. For example, if the program in question were a compiler, it is often possible to recover from an error and yield valid error information on a later section of the program. Alternately, if the program were a calculator, it would be extremely rude to quit merely because the user typed in the wrong sequence of characters. Thus, error recovery is an important element in the parser. Associated with the **error** token (and the newline token) is an action—printing out a warning message. For a full-scale compiler, this could include information on the type of error (e.g., "unterminated

---

*For those who use the ASCII character set, this means all characters from 0x00 (in hex) to 0xFF (also in hex). For those who use EBCDIC, it will depend upon your implementation of yacc.

character string" or "syntax error") and where the error occurred (perhaps the line number). Both these techniques are discussed later in more detail.

Actions

An action can be associated with a rule and consists of C code that will be executed each time the rule is matched. Actions usually manipulate the values of tokens.

The yacc-generated parser saves the values of each token in a *working variable* (**yyval** defined to be the same type as **yylval**, the variable used by the lexical analyzer to pass token values to the parser). These working variables are available to be used within the action rules; in the actual code, they are replaced with the correct internal yacc reference. The variables are labeled "$1", "$2", "$3", etc. The pseudo-variable "$$" is the value to be returned by that invocation of the rule. This is useful, for instance, when writing an interactive calculator where the result of a particular calculation can be returned by assigning the appropriate value to "$$". For instance, in the portion of the **list** rule that contains the "list object" form, "$1" will be the value of **list** and "$2" will be the value of **object**. This can be useful in a variety of contexts, such as interpreting expressions.

When an action occurs inside a rule, it may have a return value. That return value then takes a working variable and may be referenced as such. Thus, the value of **error** in the above example is "$1", the return value of the action (even if it is empty) is "$2", and the return value of the newline is "$3".

Actions may be performed *after* any member of the token set. For instance, we could have the rule:

```
list:     object
        | list object
        | error
                    { warning("unknown object",
                            (char *)0);
                      printf("resynchronizing\n"); }
          '\n'
        ;
```

For this case, the final effect is not different, but it is a useful technique for some problems.

Code Section

The third section, the code section, is where all the supporting routines are located. Of these routines, three are required: **main**, **yylex**, and **yyerror**.* Because the yacc-generated code expects to find these routines, they must either be located here or be externally linked into the executable program. In our sample yacc specification, these routines are found in *progs.c* and included from the code section.

main Routine

Look at a **main** routine for our sample program:

```
#include <stdio.h>
#include <ctype.h>
char *progname;
int lineno = 1;
int Out_lineno = 1; /* output line number */

main(argc,argv)
int argc;
char *argv[];
{
#ifdef YYDEBUG
    extern yydebug;
#endif
    double fu = 1.0;

    progname = argv[0];
#ifdef YYDEBUG
    if(argc > 1) yydebug = 1;
#endif
    return(yyparse());
}
```

main is a (deliberately) simple program. It assigns the global variable **progname** (used by warning to print out the program's name with the error message), then checks to see if debugging is desired (in this case, if there were any arguments on the command line). Debugging refers to yacc's internal debugging mechanism that identifies how the state machine is operating. It is a useful tool for debug-

---

*Default versions are available in the yacc library, but it is often necessary to write your own. On UNIX systems, the yacc library is referenced by adding **-ly** on the link line.

ging a grammar and will be discussed in greater detail later. Finally, **main** calls **yyparse**, which is the name for the yacc-generated parser. This routine calls **yylex**, the lexical analyzer.

yylex Routine

yylex tokenizes the input stream for the yacc-generated parser. Conveniently, lex generates a routine called **yylex** to work with yacc. However, in our example, a "custom" lexical analyzer has been used. The actual operation of the lexical analyzer is quite important to the final functioning of the program. If the lexical analyzer returns the wrong type of token or an incorrectly formed token, yacc will generate improper output.

Here is an example of a custom **yylex** routine that is used with the sample program:

```
yylex()
{
    int c;

    while ((c=getchar()) == ' ' || c == '\t')
        ;
    if (c == EOF)
        return 0;
    if (c == '.' || isdigit(c)) {      /* number */
        ungetc(c, stdin);
        scanf("%lf", &yylval.val);
        return NUMBER;
    }
    if ( c == '#' ) { /* comment */
        char *p = textbuf;
        int index = 1;
        do {
            if (index < sizeof(textbuf)) *p++ = c;
        } while ((c = getchar()) != EOF && c != '\n');
        ungetc(c, stdin);
        yylval.text = textbuf;
        return COMMENT;
    }

    if ( c == '"' ) { /* literal text */
        char *p = textbuf;
        int index = 1;
        while ((c = getchar()) != EOF &&
                c != '"' && c != '\n' &&
                index < sizeof(textbuf))
        {
            *p++ = c;
        }
```

```
        *p = '\0';
        if(c == '\n') ungetc(c,stdin);
        yylval.text = textbuf;
        return TEXT;
    }
    if ( isalpha(c)) { /* check to see if it is a command */
        char *p = textbuf;
        int index = 1;

        do {
            *p++ = c;
        } while ((c = getchar()) != EOF && isalnum(c));
        ungetc(c, stdin);
        *p = '\0';
        yylval.text = textbuf;
        return COMMAND;
    }
    if ( c == '\n') lineno++;
    return c;
}
```

First, this analyzer is fairly basic and could serve as the basis for a variety of simple programs. However, for a more full-scale project, it will often be more desirable to use lex. Nevertheless, this lexical analyzer illustrates the basic functionality admirably. The first action is to retrieve a character from the standard input and either throw it away if it is whitespace or begin processing it if it is not. If an EOF has been detected, 0 is returned by **yylex**, which indicates to yacc that the end of the input stream has been seen. Note that input can be terminated whenever *any* character is seen. For most applications, however, EOF is sufficient. Next, if a period or a digit is seen, the token is assumed to be a number.* Every character that could be part of the number is used, as that is how **scanf** will translate the remaining input, and is then placed into **yylval.val**, which happens to be the union field corresponding to the **NUMBER** type, as shown in the declarations section. Finally, the terminal value **NUMBER** is returned by **yylex**.

If the token is not a number or a period, it then is tested to see if it begins with a "#". If it does, all the text until the end of the line is considered a comment. It is important to note that the newline, although used to detect the end of the comment, is not destroyed. Rather, it is pushed back onto the front of the input stream. Failure to do this will change the operations of the program. You should feel free to experiment, as this will yield a greater appreciation of how such a simple change can have significant impact. Next the lexical analyzer checks to

---

*If the sample program is actually run, it is interesting to note that if a ".", is used by itself, it is identified as a number. This demonstrates that yacc is ignorant of the *true* type of the token—its *semantic* value; rather, it relies upon the lexical analyzer to report the correct token type—its *syntactic* value. It is up to the *programmer* to use the semantic value correctly. For this program, the effect of reporting "." as a number is harmless. In others, however, it could generate improper behavior.

see if the token begins with a quotation mark. If it does, the contents up to the end-of-line or second quotation mark are taken as a **TEXT** type terminal. Once again, the unused newline is pushed back into the input stream.

After exhausting the special characters, the lexical analyzer checks to see if the character is an alphabetic character. If it is, the remaining balance of alphanumeric characters constitute a **COMMAND** which, in C, could be keywords, variables, or functions. Finally, failing this test, the individual character is returned (recall that an individual character is a terminal). If the character was a newline, the line number indicator is incremented to allow for proper error reporting.

yyerror Routine

The routine **yyerror** is called by the yacc state machine whenever an error is detected. Here is the **yyerror** routine defined for our sample program:

```
yyerror(s) /* called for yacc syntax error */
char *s;
{
    warning(s, (char *)0);
}

warning(s, t)      /* print warning message */
char *s, *t;
{
    fprintf(stderr, "%s: %s", progname, s);
    if (t)
        fprintf(stderr, " %s", t);
    fprintf(stderr, " near line %\n", lineno);
}
```

It is passed a single string pointer which can be ignored (for example, when there is already an error reporting scheme in place) or used when it is passed onto the function **warning**. The function **warning** is a strictly local routine used for generating an error string. It takes two arguments and prints them in what we hope is a "superior" format to that normally used by yacc.

This concludes our description of yacc. In Chapter 8, *Ambiguities and Conflicts in Yacc Grammars*, we look at potential problems in yacc grammars. Consult Appendix B, *Yacc Options and Error Messages*, to look up error messages produced by compiling a yacc grammar.

8

Ambiguities and Conflicts in Yacc Grammars

The Pointer Model and Conflicts
Real Examples

This chapter focuses on finding and correcting *conflicts* within a yacc specification. You have conflicts when yacc reports shift/reduce and reduce/reduce errors. In this chapter, we will explain what the conflicts are and how you can find them. Finding them can be challenging because yacc points to them in *y.output*, which we will describe in this chapter, rather than in your yacc specification file. We will tell how to find your way back from *y.output* to your input file. Before reading this chapter, you should understand pushdown automata as described in Chapter 1, *Introduction to Lex and Yacc*.

The Pointer Model and Conflicts

Let's begin by describing what a conflict is in terms of the yacc specification. To do this, we must introduce a useful model of yacc's operation that controls a pointer. The pointer in this model moves through the yacc specification as each individual token is read. When you start, there is one pointer (represented here as an up-arrow, ↑) at the beginning of the starting rule:

```
%token A B C
%%
start: ↑ A B C
```

As the yacc parser reads tokens, the pointer moves. Say it reads A and B:

```
%token A B C
%%
start: A B ↑ C
```

At times, there may be more than one pointer because of the alternatives in your yacc specification. For example, suppose it reads A and B:

```
%token A B C D E F
%%
start: x | y;
x: A B ↑ C D
y: A B ↑ E F
```

For the rest of the examples in this chapter, we will leave out the **%token** and the **%%**. There are two ways for pointers to disappear. One is for a token to eliminate one or more pointers. If the next token that yacc reads is a C, then the second pointer will disappear, and the first pointer will advance:

```
start: x | y;
x: A B C ↑ D
y: A B E F
```

The other way for pointers to disappear is for them to merge in a common subrule:

```
start: x | y;
x: A B z R
y: A B z S
z: C D
```

In the description above, after A, there will be two pointers:

```
start: x | y;
x: A ↑ B z R
y: A ↑ B z S
z: C D
```

After A B C, there will only be one pointer:

```
start: x | y;
x: A B z R
y: A B z S
z: C ↑ D
```

And after A B C D, there will again be two:

```
start: x | y;
x: A B z ↑ R
y: A B z ↑ S
z: C D ↑
```

When a pointer reaches the end of a rule, the rule is *reduced*. Rule z was reduced when the pointer got to the end of it after yacc read D. Then the pointer returns to the rule from which the reduced rule was called, or as in the case above, the pointer splits up into the rules from which the reduced rule was called.

Now we can define a *conflict*. There is a conflict if a rule is reduced when there is more than one pointer. Here is an example of reductions with only one pointer:

```
start: x | y;
x: A ↑
y: B ↑
```

After A, there will only be one pointer—in rule x—and rule x will reduce. Similarly, after B, there will only be one pointer—in rule y—and rule y will reduce. Here is an example of a conflict:

```
start: x | y;
x: A ↑
y: A ↑
```

After A, there are two pointers, at the ends of rules x and y. They both want to reduce, so it is a reduce/reduce conflict.

There is no conflict if there is only one pointer, even if it is the result of merging pointers into a common subrule and even if the reduction will result in more than one pointer:

```
start: x | y;
x: z R
y: z S
z: A B ↑
```

After A B, there will be one pointer, at the end of rule z, and that rule will be reduced, resulting in two pointers:

```
start: x | y;
x: z ↑ R
y: z ↑ S
z: A B
```

But at the time of the reduction, there was only one pointer, so it is *not* a conflict.

Types of Conflicts

There are two kinds of conflicts, reduce/reduce and shift/reduce. Conflicts are categorized based upon what is happening with the other pointer when one of them is reducing. If the other rule is also reducing, it is a reduce/reduce conflict. The following example has a reduce/reduce conflict in rules x and y:

```
start: x | y;
x: A ↑
y: A ↑
```

If the other pointer is not reducing, then it is shifting, and the conflict is a *shift/reduce* conflict. For example, the following has a shift/reduce conflict in rules x and y:

```
start: x | y R
x: A ↑ R
y: A ↑
```

After yacc accepts A, rule y needs to reduce back to rule start, where R can be accepted, while rule x can accept R immediately.

If there are more than two pointers at the time of a reduce, yacc lists the conflicts in pairs. The following example has a reduce/reduce conflict in rules x and y and another reduce/reduce conflict in rules x and z, according to yacc:

```
start: x | y | z;
x: A ↑
y: A ↑
z: A ↑
```

Now we need to further define exactly when the reduction takes place with respect to token lookahead and pointers disappearing so we can keep our simple definition of conflicts correct. Here is a reduce/reduce conflict:

```
start: x B | y B
x: A ↑
y: A ↑
```

But there is no conflict here:

```
start: x B | y C
x: A ↑
y: A ↑
```

The reason the second example is not a conflict is because yacc can look ahead one token after the A. If it sees a B coming, then the pointer in rule y disappears before rule x reduces. Similarly, if it sees a C coming, the pointer in rule x disappears before rule y reduces. Yacc can only look ahead one token, though. The following is not a conflict in a compiler that can look ahead two tokens, but in yacc, it is a reduce/reduce conflict:

```
start: x B C | y B D
x: A ↑
y: A ↑
```

States and Conflicts in y.output

Rather than telling where your conflicts lie in your yacc specification, yacc tells where they are in *y.output*, which is a description of the state machine it is generating. We need to discuss what the states are, then how to find the problem in your yacc specification given a shift/reduce or reduce/reduce conflict described in *y.output*. Initially, we describe the *y.output* file. You can generate the *y.output* file by running yacc with the **-v** (verbose) option.

Each state corresponds to a unique combination of possible pointers in your yacc specification. Every nonempty yacc specification has two unique possible pointer positions: one at the beginning, when no input has been accepted, and one at the end, when a complete grammar has been accepted. The following simple example has two more:

```
start: A <one here> B <another here> C
```

For future examples, we will number the states as a clear means of identification. Although yacc numbers the states, the order of the numbers is not significant:

```
start: A <state 1> B <state 2> C
```

When a given stream of input tokens can correspond to more than one possible pointer position, then all the pointers for a given token stream correspond to one state:

```
start: a | b
a: X <state 1> Y <state 2> Z
b: X <state 1> Y <state 2> Q
```

Different input streams can correspond to the same state when they correspond to the same pointer:

```
start: threeAs;
threeAs: /* empty */ | threeAs A <state 1> A <state2>
                       A <state 3>;
```

The grammar above accepts some multiple of three 'A's. State 1 corresponds to 1, 4, 7, etc. 'A's; state 2 corresponds to 2, 5, 8, etc. 'A's; and so on. Although not as good design, we will rewrite this with right recursion in order to illustrate the next point (yacc will report conflicts otherwise):

```
start: threeAs;
threeAs: /* empty */ | A A A threeAs;
```

A position in a rule does not necessarily correspond to only one state. A given pointer in one rule can correspond to different pointers in another rule, making several states:

```
start: threeAs X | twoAs Y
threeAs: /* empty */ | A A A threeAs;
twoAs: /* empty */ | A A twoAs;
```

The grammar above accepts multiples of 2 or 3 'A's, followed by an X for multiples of 3, or a Y for multiples of 2. (Without the X or Y, the grammar would have a conflict, not knowing whether a multiple of 6 'A's satisfied threeAs or twoAs.) If we number the states as follows:

```
state 1: 1, 7, ... 'A's accepted
state 2: 2, 8, ... 'A's accepted
...
state 6: 6, 12, ... 'A's accepted
```

then the corresponding pointer positions are as follows:

```
start: threeAs X | twoAs Y;
threeAs: /* empty */ | A <1,4> A <2,5> A <3,6> threeAs;
twoAs: /* empty */ | A <1,3,5> A <2,4,6> twoAs;
```

That is, after the first A in threeAs, yacc could have accepted 6i+1 or 6i+4 'A's, where i is 0, 1, etc. Similarly, after the first A in twoAs, yacc could have accepted 6i+1, 6i+3, or 6i+5 'A's.

Now that we have demonstrated what states are, we can look at the conflicts described in *y.output* and determine what part of our yacc specification causes them:

```
start: a Y | b Y
a: X
b: X
```

The example above produces the following in *y.output*, without the numbers on the left, which we have added:

```
1.  4: reduce/reduce conflict (red'ns 3 and 4 ) on Y
2.  state 4
3.  a : X_     (3)
4.  b : X_     (4)
```

The first line states that state 4 has a reduce/reduce conflict between reduction 3 and reduction 4 when token Y is received. Lines 2 through 4 describe state 4. Lines 3 and 4 show reduction 3, which reduces rule a, and reduction 4, which reduces rule b. The underscore shows where in the rule you are before receiving the next token. This corresponds to the pointer in the yacc specification. For reduce conflicts, you will always be at the end of the rule. You should note that yacc's use of underscore to show where you are in the rule can get confusing if you have rules with underscores in them.

The rules may have tokens or rule names in them:

```
start: a Z | b Z;
a: X y;
b: X y;
y: Y

7: reduce/reduce conflict (red'ns 3 and 4 ) on Z
state 7
a :   X y_    (3)
b :   X y_    (4)
```

You can see that in the last two lines, yacc does not distinguish between tokens and rule names. This is not a problem if you use upper-case token names, as we have.

The rules do not have to be identical:

```
start: A B x Z | y Z
x: C
y: A B C

7: reduce/reduce conflict (red'ns 3 and 4 ) on Z
state 7
x :   C_     (3)
y :   A B C_    (4)
```

In state 7, yacc has already accepted A B C. Rule x only has C in it, because in the rule from which x is called, start, A B is accepted before calling x.

And now for a shift/reduce conflict:

```
start: x | y R
x: A R
y: A

4: shift/reduce conflict (shift 6, red'n 4) on R
state 4
x :   A_R
y :   A_     (4)
```

In the example above, state 4 has a shift/reduce conflict between shifting token R (and advancing to state 6) and reducing rule 4. Rule 4 is rule y, as shown in the last line:

```
y : A_      (4)
```

You can find the reduce rule in a shift/reduce conflict the same way you find both rules in a reduce/reduce conflict. The reduction number is in parentheses on the right. In the case above, the rule with the shift conflict is the only rule left in the state:

```
x: A_R
```

Yacc is in rule x, having accepted A and about to accept R. The shift conflict rule was easy to find in this case, because it is the only rule left, and it shows that the next token is R. The next thing showing may be a rule instead of a token:

```
start: x1 | x2 | y R
x1: A R
x2: A z;
y: A
z: R

5: shift/reduce conflict (shift 7, red'n 6) on R
state 5
x1 :  A_R
x2 :  A_z
y :  A_      (6)
```

In the example above, the reduction rule is:

```
y : A_      (6)
```

so that leaves two candidates for the shift conflict:

```
x1 :  A_R
x2 :  A_z
```

Rule x1 shows the next token, R, so you know it is part of the shift conflict, but rule x2 shows the next rule (not token), because that is how they appear in the yacc specification. You have to go look at the rule z to find out if the first token it wants is an R.

There could be more rules in state 5, and they may not all want the R next:

```
start: x1 | x2 | x3 | y R
x1: A R
x2: A z1;
x3: A z2;
y: A
z1: R
z2: S
```

```
6: shift/reduce conflict (shift 8, red'n 8) on R
state 6
x1 :   A_R
x2 :   A_z1
x3 :   A_z2
y  :   A_     (8)
```

In this example, rule y, or 8, is the reduce problem. x1 is obviously a shift problem, because it shows the next token to be R. It is not immediately obvious about x2 or x3, because they show rules z1 and z2 following their underscores. When you look at rules z1 and z2, you find that z1 wants an R next and z2 wants an S next, so x2 is part of the shift conflict and x3 is not.

In each of our last two shift/reduce conflict examples, can you see a reduce/reduce conflict? Run yacc and look in *y.output* to check your answer.

Review of Conflicts in y.output

Now we will review the relationship between our pointer model, conflicts, and *y.output*. First, a reduce/reduce conflict:

```
start: A B x Z | y Z
x: C
y: A B C

7: reduce/reduce conflict (red'ns 3 and 4 ) on Z
state 7
x :   C_        (3)
y :   A B C_       (4)
```

There is a conflict, because if the next token is Z, yacc wants to reduce rules 3 and 4, or x and y. Or using our pointer model, there are two pointers and both are reducing:

```
start: A B x Z | y Z
x: C ↑;
y: A B C ↑;
```

Now a shift/reduce example:

```
start: x | y R
x: A R
y: A

4: shift/reduce conflict (shift 6, red'n 4) on R
state 4
x :   A_R
y :   A_      (4)
```

There is a conflict, because if the next token is R, yacc wants to reduce rule y and shift an R in rule x. Or there are two pointers and one is reducing:

```
start: x | y R
x: A ↑ R
y: A ↑ ;
```

Real Examples

Our first example is out of the UNIX yacc manual. We have added a terminal for completeness:

```
expr: TERMINAL | expr '-' expr;

4: shift/reduce conflict (shift 3, red'n 2) on -
state 4
expr :   expr_- expr
expr :   expr - expr_     (2)
```

Yacc tells us that there is a shift/reduce conflict when you get the minus token. Adding our pointers:

```
expr: expr ↑ - expr
expr: expr - expr ↑
```

Note that they are the same rule and not even different alternatives under the same name. This shows that you can have a state where your pointers can be in two different places in the same rule. This is because of the recursiveness of the example. (In fact, all of the examples in this section are recursive. We have found that most of the tricky yacc problems are recursive.)

After accepting two **expr**'s and a minus, the pointer is at the end of rule **expr**, as shown in the second line of the pointer example above. But "expr - expr" is also an **expr**, so your pointer can also be just after the first **expr**, as shown in the first line of the example above. If the next token is not a minus, then the pointer in the first line disappears because it wants a minus next, so you are back to one pointer. But if the next token is a minus, then the second line wants to reduce, and the first line wants to shift.

If you were solving this conflict, you would look at *y.output* to find the source of the conflict:

```
4: shift/reduce conflict (shift 3, red'n 2) on -
state 4
expr :   expr_- expr
expr :   expr - expr_     (2)
```

Get rid of irrelevant rules in the state (there are not any here), and optionally picture the pointers:

```
expr: expr ↑ - expr
expr: expr - expr ↑
```

After the analysis above, it becomes clearer that the problem is:

```
expr - expr - expr
```

This expression could be interpreted using left associativity as follows:

```
(expr - expr) - expr
```

or using right associativity as follows:

```
expr - (expr - expr)
```

The problem is that after reading "expr - expr", the parser could reduce if using left associativity or shift using right associativity. If not instructed to prefer one or the other, this ambiguity causes a shift/reduce conflict.

Our next example is also out of the UNIX yacc manual. Again we have added a terminal for completeness:

```
stmt : IF '(' cond ')' stmt
 | IF '(' cond ')' stmt ELSE stmt
 | TERMINAL;
cond : TERMINAL;

8: shift/reduce conflict (shift 9, red'n 1) on ELSE
state 8
stmt :  IF ( cond ) stmt_      (1)
stmt :  IF ( cond ) stmt_ELSE stmt
```

In terms of pointers:

```
stmt: IF ( cond ) stmt ↑
stmt: IF ( cond ) stmt ↑ ELSE stmt
```

The first line is the reduce part of the conflict, and the second, the shift part. This time they are different alternatives of the same name rule. To figure out what is going wrong at a higher level, we see where the first line reduces back to. It has to be a call to **stmt**, followed by an **ELSE**. There is only one place where that can happen:

```
stmt: IF ( cond ) stmt <return to here> ELSE stmt
```

You return to the exact spot where the pointer is for the shift part of the conflict. In fact, that is the same as what was happening with "expr - expr - expr" in the previous example. And using logic similar to what you used in the previous example, in order to reduce "IF (cond) stmt" into "stmt" and end up here:

```
stmt: IF ( cond ) stmt <here> ELSE stmt
```

you have to have this token stream:

```
IF ( cond ) IF ( cond ) stmt ELSE
```

And, again, as discussed in the manual, the problem is how to group it:

```
IF ( cond ) { IF ( cond ) stmt } ELSE stmt
IF ( cond ) { IF ( cond ) stmt ELSE stmt }
```

And, again, the manual explains how to tell yacc which you want. Our goal in this chapter is to tell you how to get to the point that you understand the problem at a high enough level, so you can then fix it.

To review how to get to that point:

- Find the shift/reduce error in *y.output.*
- Pick out the reduce rule.
- Pick out the relevant shift rules.
- See where the reduce rule will reduce back to.
- With this much information, you ought to be able to deduce the token stream leading up to the conflict. Shifting and reducing will give you the grouping conflict.

Seeing where the reduce rule will reduce back to is typically as easy as we have shown. However, it is possible for a grammar to be so complicated that it is not practical to use our "hunt-around" method, and you will need to learn the detailed operation of the state machine to find the states to which you reduce.

Our final example is a simple version of a problem we have helped people track down a number of times. For some reason, novice yacc programmers seem to run into it easily:

```
start: outerlist Z
outerlist: /* empty */ | | outerlist outerlistitem;
outerlistitem: innerlist;
innerlist: /* empty */ | innerlist innerlistitem;
innerlistitem: I;
```

```
2: shift/reduce conflict (shift 3, red'n 5) on Z
state 2
start : outerlist_Z
outerlist : outerlist_outerlistitem
innerlist : _     (5)
```

Let us go through the steps. The reduce rule is the empty alternative of innerlist. That leaves two candidates for the shift problem. Rule start obviously is one, because it explicitly takes Z as the next token. The nonempty alternative of outerlist might be, if it will take token Z next. It turns out that the only way is for outerlist to take an empty innerlist, which does not seem to add much information to what we have already. To find what innerlist reduces back to, we need to see which of the calls to innerlist can be followed by token Z. The one in the nonempty alternative of innerlist is out, because it is followed by innerlistitem, which requires token I. That leaves the one in outerlistitem, which is called from the nonempty alternative of outerlist, which is called from start and is followed by token Z.

This all boils down to the parsing being in this state: we have just finished an innerlist, possibly empty, or an outerlist, possibly empty. How can it not know which list it has just finished? Look at the two list expressions. They can both be empty, and the inner one sits in the outer one without any token to say it is starting or finishing the inner loop. Say you do not have any tokens in the input stream, other than Z. Is that an empty outerloop or an outerloop with one item, an empty innerloop? The difference is whether it reduces the empty alternative in innerlist. If you had actions in there, you might have code to add the innerlist to a table. Should yacc execute it or not?

The problem here is that the grammar is redundant. You have a loop within a loop, with nothing special to separate them. You can toss one of the loops, or it might turn out you forgot some tokens in outerlistitem to separate the inner and outer loops.

Ambiguities and conflicts within the yacc grammar are just one type of coding error, although one that is problematical to find and correct. This chapter has presented some useful techniques for correcting these kinds of errors. In the chapter that follows, we will largely be looking at other sources of errors.

9

Error Reporting and Recovery
Error Reporting
Error Recovery

The previous two chapters discussed techniques for finding errors within the grammar's or lexical analyzer's specifications. In this chapter, we turn our attention to the other side of error correction/detection—how the grammar and lexical analyzer detect errors. This chapter will present some techniques that can be used to incorporate error detection and reporting into the grammar. To ground the discussion in a complete example, we will refer to the MGL defined in Chapter 4, *The MGL*.

Error Reporting

Yacc provides the simple **error** token and the **yyerror** routines which are typically sufficient for early versions of a tool. However, as any program begins to mature, especially a programming tool, it becomes important to provide better error recovery, which allows for detection of errors in the later portions of the file and better error reporting. First, we will discuss better error reporting.

Error reporting should detail as much information about the error as is possible. The default yacc error is to declare that a syntax error exists. In our examples, we typically added some mechanism for reporting the line number. This provides some information (the locality of the error) but does not say anything about other errors within the file or where in the specified line the error occurs.

First of all, it is best to begin categorizing the possible errors (perhaps building an array of errors and defining symbolic constants to identify the errors). For example, in the MGL (or the SGL), a common error is to not terminate a string. Another common error might be using the wrong type of string (e.g., quoted string instead of an id or vice versa). At a minimum, then, the MGL should report:

- General syntactic errors (e.g., a line that makes no sense).
- A nonterminated string.
- The wrong type of string (quoted instead of unquoted or vice versa).
- A premature end of file.
- Duplicate names used.

As the MGL undergoes more use, we will obtain experience on the types of errors users encounter. From this information, we can expand our list of errors to facilitate the inexperienced MGL user in more rapidly locating and correcting such errors. This initial list, however, should provide us with some examples of error reporting methods.

Our existing mechanism for reporting a syntax error on a particular line is a good one; if we cannot identify the error, we will use this fallback error to signal the user. Other more specific error conditions will then be placed where we recognize the possibility of such an error. In general, this should be enough to point out the offending line in the input file, which in turn is often enough to determine the nature of the error.

The duty for error correction does not lie with yacc alone, however. Many fundamental errors are better detected by lex. For instance, the normal quoted string matching pattern is:

```
\"[^\"\n]*\"
```

We would like to detect an unterminated quoted string, however. One initial idea might be to break this single rule into two rules:

```
\"[^\"]*\"  \"[^\n]*\"
```

But because lex matches the longest possible string, the first rule would attempt to wrap around lines until it found a new quotation mark; typically this would lead to an overflow of the lex buffers and cause the compiler to crash.

Instead, one potential solution would be to modify the normal rule to accept either a closing quotation mark or a newline and then examine the last character of the matched token. If the last character of the matched token is a quotation mark, all is well. If it *is not* a quotation mark, a warning is called:

```
qstring \"[^\"\n]*[\"\n]
%%
{qstring} { yylval.string = yytext;
  if(yylval.string[strlen(yylval.string)-1] != '"')
    warning("Unterminated character string\n",
                        (char *)0);
  return QSTRING; }
%%
```

This technique of accepting illegal input and then explicitly testing for that exact condition is a powerful one that can be used to greatly improve the error reporting of the compiler. If we had not added this rule, the compiler would have used the generic "syntax error" message; by reporting the specific error, the programmer can know precisely what to look for to correct this type of error. Later in this chapter, we will describe ways to resynchronize and attempt continuing operation over such errors.

The yacc equivalent of accepting erroneous input is demonstrated by testing for the improper use of a quoted string for an identifier and vice versa. For instance, the following MGL specification fragment should generate just such an error:

```
screen "foo"
```

It seems desirable to alert the programmer to this fundamental error rather than to assume they will be able to determine the error from the "syntax error" message; this is the type of error a beginning user makes. We will modify the yacc grammar to recognize this potential condition. To handle the wrong *type* of string, it is necessary to modify the yacc grammar to recognize the error condition and report it properly. Thus, we can introduce a nonterminal to replace the currently used terminals **QSTRING** and **ID**. Currently, the MGL has the rules:

```
screen_name:      SCREEN ID   { start_screen($2); }
                | SCREEN      { start_screen("default"); }
;

screen_terminator:    END ID   { end_screen($2); }
                    | END      { end_screen("default"); }
  ;

screen_contents:    line
    |  title line
                    | title
  ;
```

```
title:                  title title
                      | TITLE QSTRING { add_title($2); }
          ;
```

Instead, use the following rules to replace the **QSTRING** and **ID** terminals:

```
id:    ID    { $$ = $1; }
| QSTRING    { warning("String literal inappropriate",
                      (char *0);
                      $$ = (char *)0;}
;

qstring:    QSTRING   { $$ = $1; }
| ID         { warning("Non-string literal inappropriate",
                                (char *)0;
                      $$ = (char *)0;}
;
```

Now when the yacc grammar detects an improper string literal or identifier, it can better pinpoint the type of error. Neither of these actions does anything for error recovery (although they could), which emphasizes that error reporting is a different step than error recovery. Sometimes error recovery is not possible; often it is desirable to issue a warning but not to actually do any error recovery processing. For example, *pcc*, the portable C compiler, aborts when it sees an illegal character in the input stream. The compiler writers decided that there was a point when resynchronizing and continuing were not possible. However, *pcc* reports questionable assignments but does recovery, such as this sample C fragment:

```
struct passwd *pwd = getpwnam();
```

In this case, an error message is issued but processing continues.

Our last example is detection of reused names. This illustrates a type of error detection that occurs within the actual compiler code, rather than within the lexical analyzer or the grammar; indeed, it cannot be implemented inside the grammar or lexical analyzer because it requires *memory* of the tokens previously seen. Recall from Chapter 4, that the grammar is implemented with a one-stack machine. No mechanism for general storage is possible, which explains why this particular type of error must be detected by the actual compiler code. The approach we took with the MGL was straightforward. In this instance, duplicates only cause problems for names, so whenever a new name is encountered, it is "registered" in a list of used names. Prior to registration, however, we scan the list to see if the name is already registered; if it is, we can report an error that a duplicate name has been used. The full code is shown in Appendix E, *MGL Compiler Code*.

Error Recovery

We concentrated on error reporting in the previous section; in this section, we discuss the problem of error recovery. When an error is detected, the state machine is left in an ambiguous position. It is unlikely that meaningful processing can continue without some adjustment to the existing state machine stack.

First, there is no reason error recovery is necessary. Many programs do not attempt to continue once an error has been detected. For compilers, however, this is often undesirable, because there is a high cost associated with running the compiler itself. For example, a C compiler typically consists of several stages: the preprocessor, the parser, the data flow analyzer, and the code generator. Reporting an error in the parser stage and ceasing operation will require that the single problem be repaired and the process started again—but the work by the preprocessor must be duplicated. Instead it may be possible to recover from the error and continue examining the file for additional errors, terminating the compilation prior to invocation of the next stage. This technique improves the productivity of the programmer by shortening the edit-compile-test cycle, since several errors can be repaired for a particular iteration of the cycle.

Typically, error recovery becomes increasingly valuable as the compiler becomes increasingly complex. However, the issues involved in error recovery can be illustrated with a simple compiler such as the MGL.

Yacc Error Recovery

Yacc does have some provision for error recovery, provided by using the **error** token. Essentially, the error token is used to find a *synchronization point* in the grammar from which it is likely that processing can continue. Note we said *likely*. Sometimes our attempts at recovery will not remove enough of the erroneous state to continue, and the error messages will cascade. Either a point from which processing *can* continue will be reached or the entire process will be aborted.

In the MGL, we could use screens as synchronization points. For example, after seeing an erroneous token, it would discard the entire screen record away and begin processing the next screen. In Chapter 5, *The SGL*, our rule for a screen was:

```
screen:    screen_name screen_contents screen_terminator
| screen_name screen_terminator
;

screen_name:    SCREEN id { start_screen($2); }
                | SCREEN     { start_screen("default"); }
;

screen_terminator:    END id { end_screen($2); }
                      | END   { end_screen("default"); }
    ;
```

We can augment this to synchronize in the **screen** rule:

```
screen:    screen_name screen_contents screen_terminator
| screen_name screen_terminator
| screen_name error screen_terminator
  { warning("Syntax error",(char *)0); }
;

screen_name:    SCREEN id { start_screen($2); }
                | SCREEN     { start_screen("default"); }
;

screen_terminator:    END id { end_screen($2); }
                      | END   { end_screen("default"); }
    ;
```

This is the basic "trick" to error recovery—attempting to move forward in the input stream far enough that the new input is not adversely affected by the older input.

Error recovery is enhanced with proper language design. Modern programming languages use statement terminators, which serve as convenient synchronization points. For instance, when parsing a C grammar, a logical synchronizing character is the semicolon (;). Of course, error recovery will introduce other problems (such as missed declarations, etc.), but these can also be included in the overall error recovery scheme.

The potential for cascading errors caused by lost state, discarded variable declarations, for example, counters the tendency to throw away large portions of the input stream. One mechanism for counteracting the problem of cascading errors is to count the number of error messages reported and abort the compilation process when the count exceeds some arbitrary number. For example, many C compilers abort after reporting 100 errors within a file.

Like any other yacc rule, **error** can be followed by a set of actions. It would be typical at this type of point to perform garbage collection, reinitialization of data state, or other necessary "housekeeping" activities, so when recovery is accomplished, processing can continue. For example, the previous error recovery fragment from MGL might be expressed as:

```
screen:    screen_name screen_contents screen_terminator
| screen_name screen_terminator
| screen_name error
          { recover(); }
  screen_terminator
  { warning("Syntax error",(char *)0); }
;
```

Unfortunately, this means the entire input must be parsed up to a **screen_terminator** before the state machine has recovered. This means that if the screen terminator were *not* found, the entire reduction would fail, and a fatal syntax error would be encountered (recall that we have no error recovery at the level above the screen rule for this example). However, if we wish to force immediate resynchronization, the special yacc action **yyerrok** can be used. This informs the state machine that recovery has been effected and resets the parser to its normal mode. Our previous example then becomes:

```
screen:    screen_name screen_contents screen_terminator
| screen_name screen_terminator
| screen_name error
          { yyerrok; recover(); }
  screen_terminator
  { warning("Syntax error",(char *)0); }
;
```

Compiler Error Recovery

In the previous section, we described the yacc-provided mechanisms for error recovery while alluding to a programmer-supplied recovery mechanism. In this section, we will discuss such external recovery mechanisms.

The inherent difficulty with error recovery is its dependency upon semantic knowledge of the grammar rather than syntactic knowledge. This greatly complicates performing complex recovery within the grammar itself. Previously we suggested that a user-provided mechanism for resetting internal data structures of the compiler might be in order; in addition, it may be desirable for the recovery routine to actually scan the input and, using a programmer-provided heuristic, perform appropriate error recovery. For instance, a C compiler writer might decide that errors encountered during the declarations section of a code block are best recovered from by skipping the entire block rather than continuing to report additional errors. That same compiler writer might decide that errors encountered during the actual code section of the code block need only be aborted to the next semicolon. Indeed, a truly ambitious writer of compilers or interpreters might wish to report the error and attempt to describe potential correct solutions.

Once such error recovery has been performed by the compiler itself; it is necessary to flush the yacc lookahead buffer (which contains the erroneous token). This is accomplished with the built-in yacc action **yyclearin**. Yacc is then placed in a resynchronized state from which processing can continue.

Typically, sophisticated error correction will include use of both yacc error recovery for fundamental syntactic errors as well as user-provided routines for semantic errors and data structure recovery. Our final version of MGL, in Appendix E, *MGL Compiler Code*, includes some of these error recovery techniques.

A

Lex Options and Error Messages

Options
Errors Messages

Lex processes a specification file and generates source code for a lexical analyzer. By convention, the specification file has a *.l* extension. The file that lex generates is named *lex.yy.c*.

The syntax of the lex command is:

lex *options file*

where *options* is as follows:

-c   Actions are written in C (default).

-n   If table sizes for the finite state machine are set in the definitions section, the -v option is automatically invoked, printing a one-line statistical summary of the machine. Use this option to suppress printing this summary line.

-r   Actions are written in RATFOR, a dialect of FORTRAN.

-t   Source code is sent to standard output instead of to the default file *lex.yy.c*. This is useful in shell scripts that direct the output of lex to a named file.

-v   This option generates a one-line statistical summary of the finite state machine. This option is implied when any of the tables sizes are specified in the definitions section of the lex specification.

Options must be specified before the file on the command line. One or more files may be specified, but they are treated as a single specification file. Standard input is used if no file is specified.

In order to compile the lexical analyzer generated by lex, you must supply a **main** routine and two supporting routines, **yywrap** and **yyreject**. The UNIX library *libl.a* provides versions of these routines.

See Chapter 6, *A Reference for Lex Specifications*, for information on creating lex specifications.

Errors Messages

This section discusses correcting problems and errors reported by lex, aside from the shift/reduce and reduce/reduce errors discussed in Chapter 8, *Ambiguities and Conflicts in Yacc Grammars*. The error messages are organized alphabetically and are largely intended for reference use. Many of the examples show code that could generate the particular error as well as suggested methods for correcting the error condition.

Action does not terminate
While processing an action, lex encountered the end of the file before the action terminated. This is usually caused because the closing brace of the action is missing.
Solution: Terminate the action prior to the end of the file.

bad state %d %o
This is an internal lex error.
Solution: Report problem to system's software maintainer.

bad transition %d %d
This is an internal lex error.
Solution: Report problem to system's software maintainer.

Can't open %s

Lex attempted to open the output file *lex.yy.c* but was unable to do so. This is usually caused because you do not have write permission on the directory or the file exists and is not writable.

Solution: Remove the file; change permission on the directory; change directories.

Can't read input file %s

Lex was unable to open the file specified on the command line. Either the file does not exist or a file was not specified.

Solution: Invoke lex with a valid file name.

ch table needs redeclaration

While reading a %T declaration from the lex file, the number of characters defined exceeded the amount of space lex has allocated for character tables.

Solution: Either remove characters from the translation table or rebuild lex to maintain a larger translation table.

Character '%c' used twice
Character %o used twice

While processing a new translation table, a character was redeclared.

Solution: Remove the extraneous declaration.

Character value %d out of range

While processing a new translation table, an invalid character value has been seen.

Solution: Correct the invalid character value.

Definition %s not found

After seeing a {**definition**}, lex was unable to find it in the list of declared substitutions.

Solution: Replace substitution; define substitution in declarations section.

Definitions too long

Lex has a limit on the size of a definition. The length of the definition is too large.

Solution: Make the definition shorter (perhaps by breaking into two definitions); rebuild lex to allow longer definitions.

EOF inside comment

While processing a comment, lex encountered the end of the file. This is usually caused because there is an unterminated comment.

Solution: Terminate the comment prior to the end of the file.

Executable statements should occur right after %

While processing the rules section, lex saw an action without an associated regular expression. It is legal to place executable code immediately following the rules break (this code will then be executed prior to looking at the input). It is *not* legal to place such code in the rules section later. The following sample is legal:

```
%%
{ bar(); }
.  { foo(); }
```

but the lex file:

```
%%
.  { foo(); }
{ bar(); }
```

is not legal. This error is also generated when a blank line is seen between rules, for example:

```
%%
bar { bar(); }

foo { foo(); }
```

Solution: Either fix the regular expression associated with the action or move the code to the beginning of the rules section.

Extra slash removed

An invalid "/" character was removed from the input.

Solution: Remove the extra "/" character; rewrite the rule to expect a "/".

Invalid request %s

While processing the declarations section, a lex declaration (beginning with "%") was seen, but the declaration was not valid. Valid declarations are:

%{	Begins a block of C code (or RATFOR) that should be included in the final output verbatim. This code occurs early in the file, so that any external declarations here are visible within the scope of the entire file.
%a	Changes the possible number of transitions lex may use while constructing the state machine.
%c	Changes to C output.
%e	Changes the possible number of tree nodes lex may use while constructing the state machine.

%k	Changes the possible number of packed character classes lex may use while constructing the state machine.
%n	Changes the possible number of states lex may use while constructing the state machine.
%o	Toggles verbose mode (printing state at the end of the lex run).
%p	Changes the possible number of positions lex may use while constructing the state machine.
%r	Changes to RATFOR output.
%t or %T	Changes the character translation table lex uses when analyzing the input stream.

Iteration range must be positive
Can't have negative iteration

An iteration range (using {**count,count**}) was used with a negative value.
Solution: Do not use a negative value.

No space for char table reverse

While attempting to create the reversed character table, lex was unable to obtain memory from the operating system. This is caused because either lex was built improperly or the system refused to give memory to lex.
Solution: Report problem to system's software maintainer.

No translation given - null string assumed

While processing the declarations section, lex saw a substitution string that had no substitution text. It is assuming the specified string should be replaced by ε (the empty string). This is a warning message only.

Non-portable character class

While scanning through a rule, a non-portable escape sequence was specified. This occurs whenever an octal constant is used.
Solution: Live with non-portability; cease use of non-portable character constant.

Non-terminated string

While reading a rule, lex has encountered a string that does not terminate before the end of line.
Solution: Add a continuation character to the string; terminate the string with a ".

Non-terminated string or character constant
EOF in string or character constant

While processing a string, lex encountered the end of the line. This is usually caused because the closing quotation mark or marks are missing.

Solution: Terminate the string or character constant prior to the end of the line or the end of the file.

OOPS - calloc returns a 0

Lex's internal memory allocator made a call to **calloc**, and **calloc** returned 0 as the address of the new memory block (which means no memory was available). It is quite likely lex will fail to operate properly after this point.

Solution: Either lex has been improperly built or the system refused to allocate memory for lex to use. Attempt the run again; if it reoccurs, you should inform your system's software maintainer.

output table overflow

While beginning to write out the state machine, lex determined that the output table had overflowed. This is an internal lex error.

Solution: Report problem to system's software maintainer.

Parse tree too big %s

Lex has exhausted the parse tree space.

Solution: Simplify the lex specification; increase the parse tree space with the %e declaration in the declarations section.

Premature eof

While processing the declarations section, a %" was seen but no %" was seen prior to the EOF.

Solution: End the C code block prior to the end of the file.

Start conditions too long

While processing the declarations section, a start condition was seen that exceeded lex's capacity to store.

Solution: Shorten the name of the start condition.

String too long

While reading a rule, lex has encountered a string that is too long to store inside its internal (static) buffer.

Solution: Shorten the string; rewrite the string expression to use a more compact form; rebuild lex to allow larger strings.

Substitution strings may not begin with digits

While processing the declarations section, lex saw a substitution string that began with a digit. This is not valid. Example:

```
ws [ ]
3 [0-9]
```

is not a valid declarations section.

Solution: Replace the substitution string with one not beginning with a digit.

syntax error

Lex has seen a line that is syntactically incorrect.

Solution: Fix the syntax of the faulty line.

Too late for language specifier

While processing the declarations section, a **%c** or **%r** (language choice of C or RATFOR) was seen; code has already been output (via a %" %"). It is too late to change language declarations.

Solution: Declare the language earlier.

Too little core for final packing

After reading the input file and building the state machine, lex was unable to pack the final tables.

Solution: Either lex has been improperly built or the system refused to allocate memory for lex to use. Attempt the run again; if it reoccurs, run lex with the **-f** flag, which disables the final state-table packing. If the condition persists, you should inform your system's software maintainer.

Too little core for parse tree

While parsing the input file, lex has exhausted available memory.

Solution: Either lex has been improperly built or the system refused to allocate memory for lex to use. Attempt the run again; if it reoccurs, you should inform your system's software maintainer.

Too little core for state generation

After reading the input file, lex was attempting to build the state machine but was unable to allocate sufficient memory for the test.

Solution: Either lex has been improperly built or the system refused to allocate memory for lex to use. Attempt the run again; if it reoccurs, you should consult your system's software maintainer.

Too little core to begin

Lex was unable to allocate sufficient memory to begin running.

Solution: Either lex has been improperly built or the system refused to allocate memory for lex to use. Attempt the run again; if it reoccurs, you should consult your system's software maintainer.

Too many characters pushed

Lex has exhausted the stack space available for an input token.

Solution: Shorten the size of the token; rebuild lex to accept larger-sized tokens.

Too many definitions

While parsing the input file, lex has exhausted its static space for storing definitions.

Solution: Remove some definitions; rebuild lex to use a larger definitions table.

Too many large character classes

Lex has exhausted internal storage for large character classes. A large character class is used to describe the ranges that occur inside brackets ([]).

Solution: Shorten the number of different large character classes; rebuild lex to allow more large character classes.

Too many packed character classes

Lex has exhausted the space for packed character classes.

Solution: Use the %k declaration to increase the number of packed character classes allowed.

Too many positions %s

Lex has exhausted the space for positions.

Solution: Use the %p declaration to increase the number of packed character classes allowed.

Too many positions for one state - acompute

Lex has used more than 300 positions for a single state, which is an internal lex limit. This error indicates an overly complex state.

Solution: Simplify the lex specification; rebuild lex to allow more positions per state.

Too many right contexts

Lex has exhausted the space for right contexts.

Solution: Decrease the number of right contexts used; rebuild lex to allow more right contexts.

Too many start conditions

While processing the declarations section, the number of *start conditions* exceeded the size of lex's static internal table.

Solution: Remove one (or more) of the start conditions; recompile lex with a larger number of start conditions.

Too many start conditions used

Too many starting conditions were specified for a particular rule for lex to handle.

Solution: Decrease the number of starting positions; rebuild lex to allow a larger number of starting positions per rule.

Too many states %s

Lex has exhausted the space for states.

Solution: Use the %n declaration to increase the number of packed character classes allowed.

Too many transitions %s

Lex has exhausted the space for transitions.

Solution: Use the %a declaration to increase the number of packed character classes allowed.

Undefined start condition %s

A <starting condition> was seen by lex, but lex was unable to find it in the list of declared starting positions.

Solution: Replace the starting position with one that has been declared; declare the starting position in the declarations section.

Unknown option %c

Lex was invoked with an unknown switch. The valid switches are:

-c   Invokes C lex. This is the default and stems from a historical past when RATFOR lex was used.

-d   Turns on debugging of lex (if lex was compiled with LEXDEBUG defined; otherwise, this is not a valid option).

-f   Turns off "optimization" mode (it does not pack the final data structures). In general, it should not be necessary to use this option (barring space problems).

-r   Invokes RATFOR lex. Unlikely to be useful to most programmers.

> **-t** Sends lex output to the standard output (*stdout*), rather than writ-
> ing it to the file *lex.yy.c*.
>
> **-v** Turns on verbose mode. Lex prints a table of statistics after run-
> ning. A detailed explanation of the output is included in Chap-
> ter 6, *A Reference for Lex Specifications*.

yacc stack overflow

> Lex was written using a yacc grammar. The yacc-generated grammar has
> exhausted its stack space.
>
> Solution: Shorten or reorder the expressions in the lex specification;
> rebuild lex with a larger yacc stack area.

Yacc Options and Error Messages

Options
Error Messages

Yacc processes a specification file that describes a grammar and generates source code for a parser. By convention, the specification file has a *.y* extension. The file that yacc generates is named *y.tab.c*.

The syntax of the yacc command is:

yacc *options file*

where *options* is as follows:

-d   Generate header file *y.tab.h* that contains definitions of token names for use by lexical analyzer routine.

-l   Do not include **#line** constructs in the generated code. These constructs help identify offending lines in the specification file. This option should be used only after the grammar has been fully debugged.

-t   Include runtime debugging code when *y.tab.c* is compiled.

-v   Produce the file *y.output*, which is used to analyzes ambiguities and conflicts in the grammar. This file contains a description of parsing tables.

In order to compile the parser generated by yacc, you must supply a **main** routine and a supporting routine, **yyerror**. The UNIX library *liby.a* provides versions of these routines.

See Chapter 7, *A Reference for Yacc Specifications*, for information on creating yacc specifications.

Error Messages

This section discusses correcting problems and errors reported by yacc, aside from the shift/reduce and reduce/reduce errors discussed in Chapter 8, *Ambiguities and Conflicts in Yacc Grammars*. The error messages are organized alphabetically and are largely intended for reference use. Many of the examples show code that could generate the particular error as well as suggested methods for correcting the error condition.

%d rules never reduced

After completion of *closure*, one or more rules did not reduce. Yacc reports the number of rules that did not reduce.

Solution: Fix the rules that did not reduce. Sample:

```
%%
start: ;
foo: ;
```

'000' is illegal

An escape specified the null character. This cannot be used within the yacc grammar, as it is used internally by yacc.

Solution: Remove the offending escape.

action does not terminate

While copying an action from the input file, the end of file was seen.

Solution: Terminate the action prior to the end of file.

action table overflow
no space in action table

> While parsing the input file (or processing the input), yacc has overflowed the static action table.
>
> Solution: Simplify actions; recompile yacc with a larger action table; use *bison*.

bad %start construction

> The object of the %**start** directive was empty.
>
> Solution: Change the %**start** so it has an argument.

bad syntax in %type

> The type argument to a %**type** directive was not valid. This occurs because the directive had no arguments.
>
> Solution: Change the %**type** directive to have an argument. Sample:

```
%s
```

bad syntax on $¡ident¿ clause

> While reading an action, an invalid type declaration was detected.
>
> Solution: Correct the invalid type declaration either by removing the offending declaration or by fixing the type declaration.

bad syntax on first rule

> The first rule was syntactically incorrect. For example, yacc never found the colon following the first rule.
>
> Solution: Fix the first rule so that it is syntactically correct. Sample:

```
%%
start
```

bad tempfile

> The temporary file contained improper data. Either the temp file has been corrupted or yacc is broken.
>
> Solution: Rerun yacc; report problem to system's software maintainer.

cannot open input file

> Yacc attempted to open the input file specified on the command line but failed. This probably occurred because the file does not exist with the given name.
>
> Solution: Invoke yacc with the correct name; create the file.

cannot open temp file

Yacc attempted to open the *yacc.tmp* temporary file but failed. This probably occurred because the current directory was not writable or because a file *yacc.tmp* exists and is not writable.

Solution: Remove the *yacc.tmp* file or change the directory permissions.

cannot open y.output

Yacc attempted to open the *y.output* debugging file but failed. This probably occurred because the current directory was not writable or because a file *y.output* exists and is not writable.

Solution: Remove the *y.output* file or change the directory permissions.

cannot open y.tab.c

Yacc attempted to open the *y.tab.c* output file but failed. This probably occurred because the current directory was not writable or because a file *y.tab.c* exists and is not writable.

Solution: Remove the *y.tab.c* file or change the directory permissions.

cannot open y.tab.h

Yacc attempted to open the *y.tab.h* header file but failed. This probably occurred because the current directory was not writable or because a file *y.tab.h* exists and is not writable.

Solution: Remove the *y.tab.h* file or change the directory permissions.

cannot place goto %d

A serious error within yacc has occurred.

Solution: Report problem to system's software maintainer.

cannot reopen action tempfile

Yacc keeps all its actions in a temporary file called *yacc.acts*. This file has disappeared; it was probably deleted while yacc was running.

Solution: Do not delete yacc's temporary files while running yacc.

clobber of a array, pos'n %d, by %d

A serious error within yacc has occurred.

Solution: Report problem to system's software maintainer.

default action causes potential type clash

A typed rule has a production whose action is empty, thus making it possible the default returned type will clash with the declared type of the rule.

Solution: Add an explicit return value statement to the action. Sample:

```
%union{
int integer;
char *string;
}

%token NEXT FOO

%type <integer> foo;
%%
start: next | foo ;
next:   NEXT;
foo:         { $$ = 0;} | FOO ;
```

eof before %

While reading the input file, yacc failed to find the grammar section.
Solution: Add the %% before the grammar.

EOF encountered while processing %union

While reading the input file, yacc was processing a %union directive and reached the end of the file.
Solution: Close the %union directive.

EOF in string or character constant

While parsing a string or character constant, the end of the string or character constant was not seen before the end of the file.
Solution: Add the closing quotation mark or marks.

EOF inside comment

After beginning a comment, the end was not found prior to the end of the file.
Solution: Terminate the comment prior to the end of the file.

Error; failure to place state %d

A serious error within yacc has occurred.
Solution: Report problem to system's software maintainer.

illegal %prec syntax

While parsing a rule, a %prec directive was seen, but it was syntactically incorrect (there was no argument).
Solution: Correct the erroneous %prec directive. Sample:

```
%token NEXT FOO
%%
start: next | foo ;
next:   NEXT %prec ;
foo:    | FOO ;
```

illegal comment

After seeing a "/", the following character was *not* an "*", but one was expected.

Solution: Either add an "*" after the "/" or put quotation marks around the slash.

illegal nnn construction

While processing an octal character escape, an illegal input character was seen.

Solution: Correct the octal character escape.

illegal option: %c

You gave yacc an option other than those it recognizes: **-r, -o, -d, -v**. The options mean:

-d Makes yacc write a header file (*y.tab.h*) that includes definitions of tokens and their values. This file is used when needed in code outside the yacc file.

-o Invokes the yacc optimizer; this is the default, the flag is obsolete.

-r Invokes RATFOR yacc; this flag is obsolete.

-v Makes yacc write a debug file (*y.output*) that describes the yacc-generated state machine.

illegal or missing ' or ''

While parsing a string literal or character literal, yacc failed to find the closing single or double quote.

Solution: Supply the closing quotation mark or marks.

illegal rule: missing semicolon or | ?

Yacc is complaining about the syntax of a rule; perhaps an undeclared token is specified. A rule that contains a token yacc cannot understand has been seen.

Solution: Revise the rule so it does not have the illegal token. Sample:

```
%token NEXT FOO
%%
start: next | foo %   ;
next:  NEXT ;
foo:   | FOO ;
```

internal yacc error: pyield %d

This error is caused when, after resolving the nonterminals within the rules, there remain unresolved grammar rules. This is a serious problem and should never occur.

Solution: The yacc implementation is not performing correctly; report problem to system's software maintainer (if that's you, you've got some work to do).

invalid escape

A backslashed character (escape) has been seen, but the second character is not recognized as a valid escape character.

Solution: Correct the escape either by replacing the escaped character with a valid escape character or by removing the backslash (\\) from within the escape.

invalid escape
illegal reserved word: %s

While parsing an input file, yacc saw a directive it did not understand (directives begin with "%").

Solution: Do not use names beginning with "%"; fix the misspelling of a directive name; check to see if the directive is a *bison* directive, and if so, use *bison*.

item too big

In the process of building the output strings, yacc has encountered an item that is too large to fit inside its internal buffer.

Solution: Use a shorter name (this error occurs when the name of the item was quite large; in the implementation we used, 370 characters was the limit).

more than %d rules

While reading rules in from the specified grammar, yacc has overflowed the static space allocated for rules.

Solution: Simplify the grammar; recompile yacc with larger state tables; use *bison*.

must return a value, since LHS has a type

A typed rule does not return a value for one (or more) of its productions.

Solution: Add a return value by assigning an appropriate value to "$$".

Sample: See the specifications for both the MGL and the SGL for the appropriate method.

must specify type for %s

While parsing a **%token** directive, no type was specified for the directive.
Solution: Add a type.

must specify type of %d

While parsing the action portion of the rule, yacc has found a token usage
which must be typed.
Solution: Either declare the type of the token in the declarations section or
explicitly cast the type.

newline in string or char. const.

While parsing a string or character constant, the end of the string or character constant was not seen before the end of the line.
Solution: Add the closing quotation mark or marks.

nonterminal %s illegal after %prec

While parsing a rule, a **%prec** directive was seen, but it was followed by a
nonterminal.
Solution: Correct the erroneous **%prec** directive either by replacing the
nonterminal or by removing the offending statement. Sample:

```
%token NEXT FOO
%%
start: next | foo ;
next:  NEXT %prec foo ;
foo:   | FOO ;
```

nonterminal %s never derives any token string

The **%s** is replaced with the name of the token string that does not simplify.
An example of such a grammar would be:

```
start:   finish | error ;
finish:  finish end;
end:     ;
```

Solution: Rewrite the grammar to take out the offending rule. For
instance, the above grammar could be rewritten:

```
start:   end | error ;
end: ;
```

nonterminal %s not defined!

In resolving a rule, yacc has found a nonterminal used that is not defined. Note that this cannot happen because of a forward reference, since yacc does not try to resolve the rules until it has read the entire grammar. An example of a grammar that would generate this message:

```
start:/* nothing */ | finish | error ;
```

Yacc reports the line where the undefined nonterminal was used.

optimizer cannot open tempfile

The temporary file yacc uses cannot be opened.
Solution: Do not delete yacc temporary files while yacc is running.

out of space

While running through the optimizer, yacc has exhausted its static internal working space.
Solution: Simplify grammar; rebuild yacc with larger working space; use *bison*.

out of space in optimizer a array
a array overflow

While optimizing the state machine, yacc exhausted the static "a" array.
Solution: Simplify grammar; rebuild yacc with more space in the "a" array; use *bison*.

out of state space

In the process of adding a new state, the internal state table has overflowed. As with the "too many states" error, the correction is either to simplify the grammar or to modify yacc to provide more data structure space (the difference is that this error occurs prior to adding the new state to the state table).

Ratfor Yacc is dead: sorry..

You tried to use the -r flag with yacc. This flag used to invoke the RATFOR (Rational FORTRAN) mode of yacc; that is no longer supported.
Solution: Stick with C.

redeclaration of precedence of %s

The specified token has been given a precedence (by use of the %left, %right, or %nonassoc directives) and has been encountered again, giving it a higher precedence than before.
Solution: Remove one of the two offending declarations. Sample:

```
%left PLUS MINUS
%left TIMES DIVIDE
%left PLUS
%%
start: ;
```

Rule not reduced: %s

After completion of *closure* on the entire set of productions, a rule remained unreduced.

Solution: Examine the rule and rewrite so that it does reduce. This error message is reported in the *y.output* file.

syntax error

Yacc did not understand the statement on the given line number.

Solution: Fix the statement so that it is syntactically correct.

token illegal on LHS of grammar rule

A token was found on the left-hand side (LHS) of the rule on the specified line.

Solution: Correct the rule so that there is no token on the left-hand side of the rule. Sample:

```
%token FOO
%%
FOO: ;
```

too many characters in ids and literals

While processing the input file, yacc has exhausted the internal static storage for identifiers and literals.

Solution: Simplify grammar; rebuild yacc with larger static tables; use *bison.*

too many lookahead sets

An attempt to add a new lookahead set failed because the lookahead set buffer overflowed.

Solution: Simplify the grammar or rebuild yacc with more lookahead set space.

too many nonterminals, limit %d

While scanning the input grammar, yacc has found more nonterminals than can be placed into its statically defined buffer space.

Solution: Simplify the grammar; rebuild yacc with larger internal tables; use *bison.*

too many states

The internal state table has overflowed. Yacc uses static tables for some of its internal data. One of those tables is the state table. This table has no more room.

Solution: Simplify the grammar (thus, it will take fewer states); increase the number of allowed states by recompiling yacc; use *bison* (the GNU project's yacc replacement).

too many terminals, limit %d

While scanning the input grammar, yacc has found more terminals than can be placed into its statically defined buffer space.

Solution: Simplify the grammar; rebuild yacc with larger internal tables; use *bison*.

type redeclaration of nonterminal %s

The specified token has been declared (with a type) in a previous %**type** directive and has now been encountered in a %**type** directive with a different type.

Solution: Remove one of the the offending %**type** directives, choosing whichever is appropriate. Sample:

```
%union{
int integer;
char *string;
}

%type <string> foo
%type <integer> foo

%%
foo: { $$ = 0 };
```

type redeclaration of token %s

The specified token has been declared (with a type) in a previous %**token** directive and has now been encountered in a %**type** directive with a different type.

Solution: Remove either the %**type** directive with the offending token or the %**token** directive, whichever is appropriate. Sample:

```
%union{
int integer;
char *string;
}
%token <string> FOO

%type <integer> foo FOO

%%
foo: { $$ = 0 };
```

unexpected EOF before %

The file given to yacc was empty.

Solution: Put something in the file (preferably a yacc grammar).

unterminated < ... > clause

While parsing an input line, yacc began parsing a type name (within angle brackets) but never found the closing bracket.

Solution: Put in a closing bracket.

working set overflow

During computation of the *closure* of the rules, the data space for the working set overflowed.

Solution: Simplify the grammar or rebuild yacc with more working set space.

yacc state/nolook error

While examining the states with lookahead disabled, a forward reference was detected. This is a serious problem and should never occur.

Solution: The yacc implementation is not performing correctly.

C

GNU Bison
Differences

The GNU project's yacc replacement is called *bison*. Briefly, GNU (recursively, *G*nu is *N*ot *U*NIX) is the project of the Free Software Foundation and is an attempt to create a UNIX-like operating system with source code available publicly (although GNU is not *public domain*, it is freely available and has a license intended to keep it freely available). Hence, *bison* is available to anyone. For more information on how to obtain *bison*, GNU, or the Free Software Foundation, they may be reached at:

> Free Software Foundation, Inc.
> 675 Massachusetts Avenue
> Cambridge, MA 02139
> (617) 876-3296

Differences

In general, *bison* is compatible with yacc—although there are known yacc grammars that do not work properly on a recent version of *bison*. Nevertheless, *bison* can often be a boon when trying to deal with some of the problems associated with yacc, notably yacc's use of internal static buffers. *bison* uses dynamic memory rather than static memory and, hence, can often accept a yacc grammar that yacc will not.

Further, *bison* offers some minor differences that can prove to be of value:

- **%expect** can be used in the declarations section to tell *bison* to expect a certain number of shift/reduce conflicts. *bison* then refrains from reporting the number of shift/reduce conflicts if it is *exactly* this number.

- **%pure_parser** can be used in the declarations section to tell *bison* to generate a re-entrant parser (one without global variables). This is of use in interrupt-driven routines where a parser is needed. Keep in mind, though, that even if *bison* generates a re-entrant parser, the code in the actions and supporting routines must also be re-entrant.

- **%semantic_parser** and **%guard** are used in a *semantic parser*. A semantic parser is one based upon the meaning (or contents) of the token, rather than the type of the token. For this reason, this parser is more complex but provides more functionality. *bison* is distributed with *two* model parser internals (one called *bison.simple* and the other *bison.hairy*). *bison.hairy* is used for the semantic parser. *Guards* control the actions of the parser, handling reductions and errors.

- **@N** is used to maintain information about the tokens of the current rule. This information must be provided by the actions (as the rule occurs), but *bison* will then make it available via the **@N** construction. For a more detailed explanation, see the *bison* manual.

- *bison* does not write out names to *y.tab.c*. Instead it writes to *filename.tab.c* for the file *filename.y*.

D

GNU Flex

The GNU project is currently distributing a lex replacement called *flex*. For more information on the GNU project, see Appendix C, *GNU Bison*. The most significant advantage of using *flex* is that it generates faster lexical analyzers, and it does not have lex's limitations upon table size.

flex is mostly compatible with lex. This does mean that some specifications cannot be built with *flex*, but many will be able to take advantage of the significant improvements in speed available from *flex*.

flex sports the following differences:

- *flex* does not need an external library (lex, on the other hand, must be linked with the lex library by using -ll on the command line). The user, however, must supply a **main** function (or some other function which calls **yylex**).

- *flex* does not support lex's RATFOR scanners either through the command line option or through the declaration file option (%r).

- *flex* does not support lex's translation tables (via the %t or %T declaration in the lex specification file).

- *flex* expands options slightly differently than lex. Whenever an expansion is performed, it is grouped by placing parentheses, (). For example, the *flex* documentation lists the following:

```
NAME    [A-Z][A-Z0-9]*
%%
foo{NAME}?       printf( "Found it\n" );
%%
```

Lex will not match the string "foo" in this example but will match it with *flex*. Without the grouping, the last parameter of the expansion is the target of the question mark (?) operator. With the grouping, the entire expansion is the target of the "?" operator.

- There is no support for the **yymore** functionality of lex.
- The internal (undocumented) lex variable **yylineno** is not supported.
- To use **REJECT**, the **-r** flag must be specified when compiling with *flex*. **REJECT** is used in the actions for the lex rules to force continuation.
- The lex **input** and **output** functions are not supported. Instead the macro **YY_INPUT** is available for modifying input handling. Output may be redirected by modifying the *flex* file pointer **yyout**. Similarly, input may be redirected by modifying the *flex* file pointer **yyin**.
- Use of trailing contexts is restricted to patterns with a fixed leading portion or a fixed trailing portion. It is not possible to have both variable leading and variable trailing portions.
- *flex* reads only one input file; lex reads the entire list of files and concatenates the files together. This is one reason why **yywrap** is far more useful for *flex* than lex.

flex offers the following additional features:

- *flex* offers *exclusive start conditions*, that is, conditions which exclude all other conditions when in that state.
- *flex* dynamically allocates tables, so the lex table directives are not necessary.
- Internally, *flex* maintains the name of the scanning routine as a macro **YY_DECL**. If this is modified, it will use a name other than **yylex**.
- *flex* allows multiple actions on the same line (without braces, {}).
- *flex* allows use of %{ and %} in actions. In this case, it copies the entire contents of the braces to the output, rather than attempting to match braces.
- All scanner actions (ECHO, **yywrap**, etc.) are macros and may be rewritten without modifying the (external) lex library. The only exception is the function **unput**.

E

MGL Compiler Code

In Chapter 4, *The MGL*, the lex and yacc grammars for the MGL were presented. The following is a sample run-time module used in conjunction with the MGL output. It is important to remember that this is not the only way this run-time support could be implemented. It does, however, implement a simple run-time environment. Immediately obvious additions include:

- Screen clearing after improper input.

- Better handling of the **execl** (i.e., take a string, tokenize it into arguments, and pass the arguments).

- Automatic generation of a **main** routine. Currently, it must be defined outside the calling program. Further, it must call the routine **menu_cleanup** before exiting. This could be (trivially) implemented.

- Implement use of the command feature. This was intended to allow the user to type a command and access a function immediately. For example, it might be possible, from any menu, to access a particular function (say, *prime*). Then to access the *prime* program, the user need only type *prime*. This provides the flexibility of a menu-driven system with the niceties of a command-driven system.

- Currently the keyboard input is taken buffered, rather than in either *cbreak* or *raw* mode. It would be possible to handle *function keys* by using *cbreak* (or *raw*) mode and recognizing the commands as a command. Of course, this does add the overhead of dealing with valid numeric choices immediately (function keys seldom have a carriage return or a line feed after them, thus they must be recognized "on the fly").

Remember, the goal of the MGL was to demonstrate a usable program to show how lex and yacc can be used. The MGL is only a byproduct of that main goal. It is, however, an excellent base with which to create more complex systems (such as SGL). The run-time system, although important, does not affect the issues of the grammar or language description significantly.

See *Preface* for information on obtaining an on-line copy of this code.

MGL Supporting Code

```
/* subr.c */

/*
 * Supporting subroutines for the menu generation
 * language (MGL)
 *
 * Tony Mason
 * November 1988
 */

/* includes */
#include <stdio.h>
#include <sysexits.h>
#include "menu_yacc.h"
#include "subr.h"                     /* contains definitions of
                                       * skeleton file to be built */

#ifdef NOBCOPY
#define bzero(x,y) memset(x,0,y)
#endif /* NOBCOPY */

/* imports */
extern int screen_done;
extern char cmd_str[], act_str[],item_str[];

/* exports */

/* local */
static char current_screen[100]; /* reasonable? */
static int done_start_init;
```

```
static int done_end_init;
static int current_line;
struct item {
    char            *desc;      /* item description */
    char            *cmd;       /* command */
    int             action;     /* action to take */
    char            *act_str;   /* action operation */
    int             attribute;  /* visible/invisible */
    struct item     *next;      /* next member of list */
  } ItemList;

/* declarations */
char *calloc(),*realloc();

/* macros */
#define SCREEN_SIZE 80
#define ALLOC(x,s,t) do { x = (t)calloc(1,(s));\
                if (x == 0)\
                { warning("memory allocation failed",\
                        (char *)0);\
                  exit(EX_OSERR); } } while(0)
#define REALLOC(x,s,t) do { x = (t)realloc(x,(s));\
                if (x == 0)\
                { warning("memory allocation failed",\
                        (char *)0);\
                  exit(EX_OSERR); } } while(0)
#define FREE(x) do { if (x) free(x); } while(0)

/* code */

/*
 * start_screen:
 * This routine begins preparation of the screen.  It
 * writes the preamble and modifies the global state
 * variable screen_done to show that a screen is in
 * progress (thus, if a screen is in progress when EOF
 * is seen, an appropriate error message can be given).
 */

start_screen(name)
  char *name;   /* name of screen to create */
  {
    long time(),tm = time((long *)0);
    char *ctime();

    if(!done_start_init)
      {
        printf("/*\n * Generated by MGL: %s */\n\n",
                ctime(&tm));
        dump_data(screen_init);
        done_start_init = 1;
      }
    if(check_name(name) == 0)
```

```
        warning("Reuse of name",name);
    printf("/* screen %s */\n", name);
    printf("menu_%s()\n{\n",name);
    printf("\textern struct item menu_%s_items[];\n\n",name);
    printf("\tif(!init) menu_init();\n\n");
    printf("\tclear();\n\trefresh();\n");

    if(strlen(name) > sizeof current_screen)
    warning("Screen name is larger than buffer",(char *)0);
    bzero(current_screen,sizeof current_screen);
    strncpy(current_screen, name, sizeof(current_screen) - 1);

    screen_done - 0;
    current_line = 0;

    return 0;
}

/*
 * add_title:
 * Add centered text to screen code.
 */
add_title(line)
    char *line;
{
    int length = strlen(line);
    int space = (SCREEN_SIZE - length) / 2;

    printf("\tmove(%d,%d);\n",current_line, space);
    current_line++;
    printf("\taddstr(%s);\n",line);
    printf("\trefresh();\n");
}

/*
 * add_line:
 * Add a line to the actions table.  It will be written
 * out after all lines have been added.  Note that some
 * of the information is in global variables.
 */

add_line(action, attrib)
    int action, attrib;
{
    struct item *new;

    ALLOC(new,sizeof(struct item),struct item *);

    new->next = ItemList.next;   /* insert at top of list */
    ItemList.next = new;

    ALLOC(new->desc,strlen(item_str) + 1,char *);
    strcpy(new->desc,item_str);
```

```
    ALLOC(new->cmd, strlen(cmd_str)+1,char *);
    strcpy(new->cmd, cmd_str);

    new->action = action;

    switch(action)
       {
    case EXECUTE:
        if(act_str[strlen(act_str)-1] == '"')
            act_str[strlen(act_str)-1] = '\0';
        /* strip trailing " */

        ALLOC(new->act_str,strlen(act_str)+1,char *);
        strcpy(new->act_str,&act_str[1]);
        /* strip leading " */
        break;
    case MENU:
        ALLOC(new->act_str,strlen(act_str)+1,char *);
        strcpy(new->act_str,act_str);
        break;
    default:
        new->act_str = 0;
        break;
       }
    new->attribute = attrib;

   }

   /*
    * end_screen:
    * Finish screen, print out postamble.
    */
end_screen(name)
   char *name;
   {

    printf("\tmenu_runtime(menu_%s_items);\n",name);

    if(strcmp(current_screen,name) != 0)
       {
        warning("name mismatch at end of screen",
                (char *)0);
       }
    printf("}\n");
    printf("/* end %s */\n",current_screen);

    process_items();

    /* write initialization code out to file */
    if(!done_end_init)
       {
```

```
          done_end_init = 1;
          dump_data(menu_init);
      }

   bzero(current_screen, sizeof current_screen);

   screen_done = 1;

   return 0;
 }

/*
 * process_items:
 * Walk the list of menu items and write them to an
 * external initialized array.  Also defines the symbolic
 * constant used for the run-time support module (which
 * is below this table).
 */
process_items()
   {
      int cnt = 0;
      struct item *ptr;

      if(ItemList.next == 0)
      return; /* nothing to do */
      printf("struct item menu_%s_items[]={\n",current_screen);
      ptr = ItemList.next;

      /* climb through the list */
      while(ptr)
         {
            if(ptr->action == MENU)
                printf("{%s,\"%s\",%d,\"\",%s,%d},\n",
                       ptr->desc,ptr->cmd, ptr->action,
                       ptr->act_str,ptr->attribute);
            else
                printf("{%s,\"%s\",%d,\"%s\",0,%d},\n",
                       ptr->desc,ptr->cmd, ptr->action,
                       ptr->act_str ? ptr->act_str : "",
                       ptr->attribute);

            FREE(ptr->desc);
            FREE(ptr->cmd);
            FREE(ptr->act_str);
            ptr = ptr->next;
            FREE(ptr);
            cnt++;
         }
      printf("{ (char *)0,  (char *)0, 0, (char *)0, 0, 0},\n");
      printf("};\n\n");
      ItemList.next = 0;

      /* now the run-time module that does all the "work" */;
```

```
   }
/*
 * This routine takes a null-terminated list of strings
 * and prints them on the standard out.  Its sole purpose
 * in life is to dump the big static arrays making up the
 * runtime code for the menus generated.
 */

dump_data(array)
   char **array;
   {
      while(*array)
         printf("%s",*array++);
   }


/*
 * this routine writes out the run-time support
 */

end_file()
  {
      static ef_called = 0;

      if(ef_called)
        {
           warning("Internal error: end_file called twice\n");
           exit(EX_SOFTWARE);
        }
      ef_called = 1;

      dump_data(menu_runtime);
  }

/*
 * Check a name to see if it has already been used.  If
 * not, return 1; otherwise, return 0.  This routine also
 * squirrels away the name for future reference.  Note
 * that this routine is purely dynamic.  It would be
 * easier to just set up a static array, but less flexible.
 */

check_name(name)
    char *name;
  {
     static char **names = 0;
     static name_count = 0;
     char **ptr,*newstr;

     if(!names)
        {
```

```
            ALLOC(names,sizeof(char *),char **);
            *names = 0;
        }

    ptr = names;
    while(*ptr)
        {
            if(strcmp(name,*ptr++) == 0) return 0;
        }

    /* not in use */
    name_count++;
    REALLOC(names, ((name_count+1) * sizeof(char *)),
            char **);
    *(names+name_count) = (char *)0;
    ALLOC(newstr,strlen(name)+1,char *);
    strcpy(newstr,name);
    *(names+name_count-1) = newstr;
    return 1;
    }

/* subr.h */

/*
 * MGL Runtime support code
 */

char *screen_init[] = {
"/* initialization information */\n",
"static int init;\n\n",
"#include <curses.h>\n",
"#include <sys/signal.h>\n",
"#include <ctype.h>\n",
"#include <sysexits.h>\n",
"#include \"menu_yacc.h\"\n\n",
"/* structure used to store menu items */\n",
"struct item {\n",
"\tchar *desc;\n",
"\tchar *cmd;\n",
"\tint  action;\n",
"\tchar    *act_str;      /* execute string */\n",
"\tint (*act_menu)();    /* call appropriate function */\n",
"\tint  attribute;\n",
"};\n\n",
0,
};

char *menu_init[] = {
"menu_init()\n",
"{\n",
"\tint menu_cleanup();\n\n",
"\tsignal(SIGINT, menu_cleanup);\n",
"\tinitscr();\n",
```

```
"\tcrmode();\n",
"}\n\n\n",
"menu_cleanup()\n",
"{\n",
"\tmvcur(0, COLS - 1, LINES - 1, 0);\n",
"\tendwin();\n",
"}\n\n",
0,
};

char *menu_runtime[] = {
"/* runtime */\n\n",
"menu_runtime(items)\n",
"    struct item *items;\n",
"    {\n",
"    unsigned count,visible,invisible,index;\n",
"    struct item *ptr;\n",
"    char buf[BUFSIZ];\n",
"    unsigned choice = 0;\n\n",
"    for(ptr = items; ptr->desc != 0; ptr++)\n",
"\tif(ptr->attribute == VISIBLE) visible++;\n",
"        else invisible++;\n\n",
"    count = visible+invisible;\n",
"    for(ptr = items,index = 1; ptr->desc != 0; ptr++,\
index++) {\n",
"        addch(\'\\n\'); /* skip a line */\n",
"\tprintw(\"\\t%d) %s\",index,ptr->desc);\n",
"        }\n\n",
"    addstr(\"\\n\\n\\t\"); /* tab out so it looks\
\"nice\"*/\n",
"    refresh();\n\n",
"    while(1)\n",
"        {\n",
"\t   while(1)\n",
"\t       {\n",
"\t\t   getstr(buf);\n\n",
"\t\t   /*\n",
"\t\t    * Check for a valid response.  It must be\
either:\n",
"\t\t    * (a) a numeric choice within the visible\
range or\n",
"\t\t    * (b) a command matching one in the list.\n",
"\t\t    */\n\n",
"\t\t   sscanf(buf,\"%d\\n\",&choice);\n",
"\t\t   if(choice > 0 && choice <= visible)\n",
"\t\t       break;\n",
"\t       }\n\n",
"\tif(choice != 0) /* numeric choice */\n",
"\t   {\n",
"\t   int i;\n\n",
"\t   for(i = 1, ptr = items; ptr->desc != 0 && i <\
choice; ptr++)\n",
"\t\t   if(ptr->attribute == VISIBLE) i++;\n",
```

```
"\t      if(ptr->attribute != 0) /* valid choice */\n",
"\t\t{\n",
"\t\t    switch(ptr->action)\n",
"\t\t       {\n",
"\t\t       case QUIT:\n",
"\t\t\t   return 0;\n",
"\t\t        case IGNORE:\n",
"\t\t\t   refresh();\n",
"\t\t\t   break;\n",

"\t\t        case EXECUTE:\n",
"\t\t\t   refresh();\n",
"\t\t\t   execl(ptr->act_str,0);\n",
"\t\t\t   break;\n",
"\t\t        case MENU:\n",
"\t\t\t   refresh();\n",
"\t\t\t   (*ptr->act_menu)();\n",
"\t\t\t   break;\n",
"\t\t         default:\n",
"\t\t\t   printw(\"default case, no action\\n\");\n",
"\t\t\t   refresh();\n",
"\t\t\t   break;\n",
"\t\t       }\n",
"\t         }\n",
"\t  }\n",
"\t  refresh();\n",
"          }\n",
"  }\n\n",
"#define ALLOC(x,s,t) do { x = (t)calloc(1,(s));\
if (x == 0)\\\n",
"\t\t\t   { fprintf(stderr,\"memory allocation \
failed\",\\\n",
"\t\t\t   (char *)0); exit(EX_OSERR); } } \
while(0)\n\n",
"casecmp(string1,string2)\n",
"    char *string1,*string2;\n",
"    {\n",
"    char *p,*q,*r;\n",
"    int result;\n\n",
"    ALLOC(p,strlen(string1)+1,char *);\n",
"    ALLOC(q,strlen(string2)+1,char *);\n\n",
"    strcpy(string1,p);\n",
"    strcpy(string2,q);\n\n",
"    for(r = p; *r != 0; r++)\n",
"        *r = (isupper(*r) ? tolower(*r) : *r);\n\n",
"    for(r = q; *r != 0; r++)\n",
"        *r = (isupper(*r) ? tolower(*r) : *r);\n\n",
"    result = strcmp(p,q);\n",
"    free(p);\n",
"    free(q);\n",
"    return result;\n",
"    }\n",
0,
};
```

MGL Yacc Grammar

```
%{
#include <stdio.h>
#define YYDEBUG 1

    int screen_done = 1; /* 1 if done, 0 otherwise */
    FILE *out;           /* output file */
    FILE *in;            /* input file */
    char act_str[256];   /* extra argument for an action */
    char cmd_str[256];   /* extra argument for command */
    char item_str[256];  /* extra argument for
                          * item description */

#ifdef NOBCOPY
#define bzero(x,y) memset(x,0,y)
#endif /* NOBCOPY */

%}

%union {
    double  real;        /* real value */
    int     integer;     /* integer value */
    char    *string;     /* string buffer */
    int     cmd;         /* command value */
}

%token <real> REAL
%token <integer> INTEGER
%token <string> QSTRING ID COMMENT
%token <cmd> SCREEN TITLE ITEM COMMAND ACTION EXECUTE EMPTY
%token <cmd> MENU QUIT IGNORE ATTRIBUTE VISIBLE INVISIBLE END

%type <cmd> action line attribute command
%type <string> id qstring

%start screens

%%

screens:  /* nothing */
        | screens screen
        | error     { warning("syntax error",(char *)0);
                    yyclearin; }
        ;
```

```
screen:     screen_name screen_contents screen_terminator
          | screen_name screen_terminator
          | screen_name error screen_terminator
                { warning("Syntax error",(char *)0);
                  yyerrok; }
          ;

screen_name: SCREEN id { start_screen($2); }
           | SCREEN    { start_screen("default"); }
           ;

screen_terminator: END id { end_screen($2); }
                 | END { end_scrcon("default"); }
                 ;

screen_contents: titles lines
               ;

titles: /* empty */
      | titles title
      ;

title: TITLE qstring { add_title($2); }
     ;

lines: /* empty */
     | lines line
     ;

line: ITEM qstring {
        if(strlen($2) > sizeof(item_str))
   warning("item string overflow",
   (char *)0);
        bzero(item_str, sizeof item_str);
        strncpy(item_str,$2, sizeof item_str);
        }
      command ACTION action attribute
      { add_line($6, $7);
        $$ = $1; }
      ;


command: /* empty */
         { bzero(cmd_str, sizeof cmd_str);
           $$ = EMPTY;}
       | COMMAND id
         { if (strlen($2) > sizeof cmd_str)
             warning("command string overflow",
                     (char *)0);
           bzero(cmd_str,sizeof cmd_str);
           strncpy(cmd_str, $2, sizeof cmd_str);
           $$ = $1; }
```

```
action: EXECUTE qstring
          { if (strlen($2) > sizeof act_str)
                warning("action string overflow",
                        (char *)0);
                bzero(act_str,sizeof act_str);
                strncpy(act_str, $2, sizeof act_str);
                $$ = $1; }
      | MENU id
          { if (strlen($2) > (sizeof(act_str) - 5))
                warning("action string overflow",
                        (char *)0);
                bzero(act_str,sizeof act_str);
                strcpy(act_str,"menu_");
                strncat(act_str, $2, sizeof(act_str)-5);
                $$ = $1; }
      | QUIT   { $$ = $1; }
      | IGNORE { $$ = $1; }
        ;

attribute: /* empty */      { $$ = VISIBLE; }
         | ATTRIBUTE VISIBLE { $$ = $2; }
         | ATTRIBUTE INVISIBLE { $$ = $2; }
           ;

id: ID
      { $$ = $1; }
   | QSTRING
      { warning("String literal inappropriate",
                (char *)0);}
    ;

qstring: QSTRING { $$ = $1; }
        | ID
            { warning("Non-string literal inappropriate",
                      (char *)0);}
          ;
%%

char *progname = "menugen";
int lineno = 1;

#include "menu_lex.c"
#include <sysexits.h>

#define DEFAULT_OUTFILE "screen.out"

char *usage = "%s: usage <outfile> <infile>\n";

main(argc,argv)
    int argc;
    char **argv;
  {
    char *outfile;
```

```
        char *infile;

        progname = argv[0];

        if(argc > 3)
            {
               fprintf(stderr,usage, progname);
               exit(EX_USAGE);
            }
        if(argc > 1)
            {
               outfile = argv[1];
               if(argc > 2)
                   {
                      infile = argv[2];
                      /* open for read */
                      in = freopen(infile,"r",stdin);
                      if(in == NULL) /* open failed */
                          {
                             fprintf(stderr,"%s: cannot open %s\n",
                                     progname, infile);
                      exit(EX_NOINPUT);
                          }
                   }
               else in = stdin;
            }
        else
            {
               outfile = DEFAULT_OUTFILE;
               in = stdin;
            }
        out = freopen(outfile,"w",stdout);
        if(out == NULL) /* open failed */
            {
               fprintf(stderr,"%s: cannot open %s\n",
                       progname, outfile);
               exit(EX_CANTCREAT);
            }

        /* normal interaction on stdin and stdout
         * from now on... */

        yyparse();

        end_file(); /* write out any final information */

        /* tidy up */
        fclose(out);
        fclose(in);

        /* now check EOF condition */
        if(!screen_done) /* in the middle of a screen */
            {
```

```
        warning("Premature EOF",(char *)0);
        unlink(outfile); /* remove bad file */
        exit(EX_DATAERR);
      }
    exit(0); /* no error */
  }

warning(s,t) /* print warning message */
  char *s, *t;
  {
    fprintf(stderr, "%s: %s", progname, s);
    if (t)
            fprintf(stderr, " %s", t);
    fprintf(stderr, " line %d\n", lineno);
  }
```

MGL Lex Specification

```
ws         [ \t]+
real       [0-9]+.[0-9]+
integer    [0-9]+
comment    ^#*$
qstring    \"[^\"\n]*[\"\n]
id         [a-zA-Z][a-zA-Z0-9]*
nl         \n

%%

{ws} ;
{real}     { sscanf(yytext,"%lf",&yylval.real);
             return REAL; }
{integer}  { sscanf(yytext,"%d", &yylval.integer);
             return INTEGER; }
{comment}  { yylval.string = yytext;
             return COMMENT; }
{qstring}  { yylval.string = yytext;
             if(yylval.string[strlen(yylval.string)-1] != '"')
              warning("Unterminated character string",(char *)0);
             return QSTRING; }
screen     { yylval.cmd = SCREEN;
             return yylval.cmd; }
title      { yylval.cmd = TITLE;
             return yylval.cmd; }
item       { yylval.cmd = ITEM;
             return yylval.cmd; }
command    { yylval.cmd = COMMAND;
             return yylval.cmd; }
action     { yylval.cmd = ACTION;
             return yylval.cmd; }
```

```
execute    { yylval.cmd = EXECUTE;
             return yylval.cmd; }
menu       { yylval.cmd = MENU;
             return yylval.cmd; }
quit       { yylval.cmd = QUIT;
             return yylval.cmd; }
ignore     { yylval.cmd = IGNORE;
             return yylval.cmd; }
attribute  { yylval.cmd = ATTRIBUTE;
             return yylval.cmd; }
visible    { yylval.cmd = VISIBLE;
             return yylval.cmd; }
invisible  { yylval.cmd = INVISIBLE;
             return yylval.cmd; }
end        { yylval.cmd = END;
             return yylval.cmd; }
{id}       { yylval.string = yytext;
             return ID;}
{nl}       { lineno++; }
.          { return yytext[0]; }
%%
```

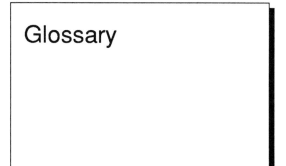

Glossary

There are a large number of technical terms used in this manual. Many of them may be familiar; some may not. To help avoid confusion, the most significant terms are listed here.

alphabet

A set of distinct symbols. For example, the ASCII character set is a collection of 128 different symbols. The state of a digital computer's memory can be represented as a two-character alphabet "0,1". All larger alphabets can be represented by this small "0,1" alphabet, so it is typically used in formal discussions because of its simplicity.

ambiguity

An uncertainty as to how a particular rule is to be interpreted is termed an *ambiguity*. For a yacc grammar, such ambiguities are classed as either *shift/reduce* or *reduce/reduce* conflicts. A shift/reduce conflict is one in which one choice is to *shift* a token onto the stack and the other choice is to *reduce* a rule; in this case, the reduction is chosen. A reduce/reduce conflict is one in which the choice is between two reductions; in this case, the reduction occurring earlier in the file is chosen. Those conflicts which cannot be resolved and are inherent to the grammar are termed *ambiguities*.

ASCII

American *S*tandard *C*ode for *I*nformation *I*nterchange; a collection of 128 symbols representing the common symbols found in the American alphabet, e.g., lower- and upper-case letters, digits, and punctuation, plus some additional characters useful in data representations, e.g., control characters.

BNF

*B*ackus-*N*aur *F*ormalism; a method of representing grammars. It is commonly used to specify formal grammars of programming languages. Yacc, the UNIX parser generator, uses a BNF-like syntax for its specification language.

BSD

*B*erkeley *S*oftware *D*istribution. The University of California at Berkeley issued a series of operating system distributions based upon UNIX Version 7; typically, BSD is also found with the version number of the particular distribution, e.g., BSD 2.10 or BSD 4.3.

compiler

A program which converts a specific representation of a set of instructions into some other representation; typically, the final goal of using a compiler is to obtain a *program* which can be executed by a computer.

conflict

An error within the yacc grammar in which two (or more) actions are possible when parsing the same input token; there are two types of conflicts: *shift/reduce* and *reduce/reduce*. (See also **ambiguity**.)

debugging

The process of locating errors within a program; for a compiler writer, this includes both locating errors within the compiler as well as providing reasonable information to the *user* of the compiler to assist that user in location of his/her own errors.

empty string

The special case of a string with zero symbols. In formal discussions, this is typically denoted as ε. In the C language, a string which consists only of the ASCII character NULL.

executable program

A program which can be executed by some existing computer.

finite automaton

An abstract machine which consists of a finite number of instructions (or *transitions*). Finite automata are useful in modeling many commonly occurring computer processes and have beneficial mathematical properties.

input

A stream of the desired type of data; typically, this is either a *byte stream* or a *record stream*, where a byte stream is a single, contiguous collection of characters and a record stream is a collection of one or more groups of characters. For instance, lex presumes its input is a byte stream, while yacc presumes its input is a *token stream* (a form of record stream).

interpreter

A program which interprets an instruction and acts upon that instruction; typically, the final goal of using an interpreter is to perform some rudimentary operation for the user.

language

Formally, a well-defined set of strings over some alphabet; informally, some set of instructions for describing abstract tasks which can then be translated into the specific language of a computer for execution.

LALR(1)

*L*ook*A*head *L*eft *R*ecursive; the (1) denotes that the lookahead is limited to a single token.

lexical analyzer

A program which converts a *byte stream* into a *token stream*. Lex takes a description of individual tokens as regular expressions and builds a state machine which recognizes those regular expressions.

LHS

*L*eft *H*and *S*ide; a commonly used shorthand mechanism for describing the *name* of some rule (e.g., a production rule).

operating system

The provider of fundamental services for the computer; it acts as a model of an abstract machine for the applications programmer, which allows for programs to be described in a high-level syntax with the specific details of translation handled by the operating system. UNIX is an example of an operating system.

nonterminals
> See **rules**.

parsing
> The process of taking a stream of *tokens* and logically grouping them into *statements* within some language.

precedence
> The order in which some particular operation is performed; e.g., when interpreting mathematical statements, multiplication and division are assigned higher precedence than addition and subtraction; thus, the statement "3+4*5" is 23 as opposed to 35.

production rules
> The rules of how statements within a particular grammar are produced. Often such production rules are written in BNF format (see also **BNF**). A yacc grammar consists of a set of production rules describing individual statements within the grammar (see also **rules**).

program
> A set of instructions, typically for a particular type of computer, which, when carried out, perform a certain predefined task. Samples of *programs* would be a compiler or an interpreter. Often such instructions must be transformed from an abstract language into the language of the particular computer.

prototyping
> The process of creating a model; lex and yacc allow the programmer to quickly construct a simple compiler, which can in turn be radically modified to observe the effects.

rules
> In yacc terminology, *rules* are the abstract description of the grammar. In lex terminology, *rules* are the regular expressions denoting tokens within the language.

semantic
> Each *token* in a yacc grammar has both a *syntactic* and a *semantic* value; its semantic value is the actual data contents of the token. For instance, the syntactic type of a certain operation may be called **INTEGER**, but its semantic value might be 3.

stream

A logical method for providing input and/or output to a particular computer program. For example, a user types at a keyboard in random spurts, but these must be provided to the applications program as if they were a continuous stream of characters. Two types of streams would be a *byte stream*, where the input appears as a collection of individual characters (as in the keyboard example), or a *record stream*, where input appears as some block of characters.

string

Formally, a series of characters over some alphabet; in the C language's representation, a series of ASCII characters terminated with the ASCII character NULL.

symbol table

A table containing specific tokens; typically, symbols are names representing some abstract object, e.g., a variable, a function, or, as in the MGL case, a menu name.

symbolic constants

In C, a *symbolic constant* is a value which is fixed at compile time but is represented within the program text as a name. The accepted practice is to represent symbolic constants in upper case; lex and yacc communicate the value of various tokens by describing them as symbolic constants; thus, when there is a **%token** statement in yacc, a corresponding symbolic constant is generated for the resulting parser.

syntactic

Each *token* in a yacc grammar has both a *semantic* and a *syntactic* value; its syntactic value is the grammatical type of the token. For instance, the semantic type of a certain operation may be 3, but its syntactic value might instead be **INTEGER**.

System V

Since the release of UNIX Version 7 (upon which the so-called BSD distributions of UNIX are based), AT&T has released several newer versions of its UNIX operating system, the most recent of which is called System V; newer versions bear release numbers, so it is common to refer to either System V, Version 4.0, or even System V.4.

terminals

In yacc terminology, *terminals* are atomic units returned by the lexical analyzer; logically, they are equivalent to any single pattern which the lexical analyzer would match as a word in the language. They are distinguished from *nonterminals*, which are defined by the parser.

token

In yacc terminology, *tokens* are either *terminals* (see also **terminals**) or *nonterminals*. In the production rules for the grammar, any name found on the right-hand side of a rule is always a token.

tokenizing

The process of converting a byte stream into a token stream is termed *tokenizing*. This is typically performed by the lexical analyzer, such as is generated by lex.

Turing machine

An abstract machine, credited to the mathematician Alan Turing, which consists of a finite set of instructions and two read/write data stores (e.g., stacks, tapes, etc.). Modern computers are functionally equivalent to the class of Turing machines known as *deterministic* Turing machines.

UNIX

The operating system developed by AT&T, and the basis of many operating systems now marketed by computer vendors. (See also **operating system**.)

yacc

*Y*et *A*nother *C*ompiler *C*ompiler; a program used for the generation of a parser from a description in BNF format.

Bibliography

Aho, Alfred V., and Ravi Sethi and Jeffrey D. Ullman. *Compilers: Principles, Techniques, and Tools.* Addison-Wesley. 1988.

Deloria. "Practical Yacc: A Gentle Introduction to the Power of this Famous Parser Generator." *The C User's Journal.* November 1987, p. 18; December/January 1988, p. 44; March/April 1988, p. 25; June/July 1988, p. 17; September/October 1988, p. 63.

Hopcroft and Jeffrey D. Ullman. *Introduction to Automata Theory, Languages, and Computation.* Addison-Wesley. 1979.

Johnson, Steven. "Yacc: Yet Another Compiler Compiler." *UNIX Programmer's Manual: Supplementary Documents 1.* University of California, Berkeley, CSRG. 1986.

Kernighan, Brian W., and Robert Pike. *The UNIX Programming Environment.* Prentice-Hall. 1984.

------ and Dennis M. Ritchie. *The C Programming Language.* Prentice-Hall. 1st Edition, 1978. 2nd Edition, 1988.

Lesk and Schmidt. "Lex — A Lexical Analyzer Generator." *UNIX Programmer's Manual: Supplementary Documents 1*. University of California, Berkeley, CSRG. 1986.

Taylor, Dave. "Interpreter Design and Construction." *Computer Language*. December 1985, p. 35; September 1986, p. 35.

Wirth, Nicklaus. *Programming in Modula-2*. Springer-Verlag. 3rd Edition, 1985.

Index

%% 22

About the Authors

Tony Mason is currently a member of the AFS development team at TRANSARC Corporation, a small start-up company specializing in distributed systems software. Previously, he worked with the Distributed Systems Group at Stanford University in the area of distributed operating systems and data communications. He received a B.S. in Mathematics from the University of Chicago in 1987.

Doug Brown has been developing software for circuit simulation, synthesis, and testing for 15 years. He is currently working on functional board test at Test Systems Strategies Inc. in Beaverton, Oregon. He received an M.S. in Electrical Engineering from the University of Illinois at Urbana-Champaign in 1976.

Colophon

Our look is the result of reader comments, our own experimentation, and distribution channels.

Distinctive covers complement our distinctive approach to UNIX documentation, breathing personality and life into potentially dry subjects. UNIX and its attendant programs can be unruly beasts. Nutshell Handbooks help you tame them.

The animals featured on the cover of *lex & yacc* are Victorian crowned pigeons.

Edie Freedman designed this cover and the entire UNIX bestiary that appears on other Nutshell Handbooks. The beasts themselves are adapted from 19th-century engravings from the Dover Pictorial Archive.

Linda Lamb designed the page layout for the Nutshell Handbooks. The text of this book is set in Times Roman; headings are Helvetica®; examples are Courier. Text was prepared using SoftQuad's *sqtroff* formatter. Figures are produced with a Macintosh™. Printing is done on an Apple LaserWriter®.

O'Reilly & Associates, Inc.

Creators and Publishers of Nutshell Handbooks,
concise, down-to-earth guides on selected UNIX topics

Basic UNIX Books:

*Learning the UNIX Operating
System*
DOS meets UNIX
Learning the vi Editor

Quick References:

UNIX in a Nutshell, System V
UNIX in a Nutshell, Berkeley

UNIX Communications:

*!%@:: A Directory of Electronic
Mail Addressing and Networks*
Using UUCP and Usenet
Managing UUCP and Usenet

UNIX and
C Programming:

Using C on the UNIX System
Lex and Yacc
Checking C Programs with lint
Understanding and Using COFF
Programming with curses
Managing Projects with make
*UNIX for FORTRAN
Programmers*

UNIX terminals:

termcap and terminfo

Send me more
information on:

❏ O'Reilly catalog and newsletter
❏ Placing a standing order for new
titles
❏ Retail sales
❏ Corporate sales
❏ Bookstore locations
❏ Overseas distributors
❏ Upcoming books on the subject:

_____

_____

❏ Writing a Nutshell Handbook

NAME

COMPANY

ADDRESS

CITY _____ STATE _____ ZIP _____

BUSINESS REPLY MAIL

FIRST CLASS MAIL   PERMIT NO. 80   SEBASTOPOL, CA

POSTAGE WILL BE PAID BY ADDRESSEE

O'Reilly & Associates, Inc.

632 Petaluma Avenue
Sebastopol, CA 95472-9902